MW00827459

Iphelia
Awakening
The Gift of Feeling

Written and Illustrated by
Erick Kenneth French

TYRIAN PRESS
Saint Louis, Missouri

TYRIAN PRESS

Iphelia: Awakening the Gift of Feeling

Disclaimer

Published in Saint Louis, MO, by Tyrian Press, LLC.
For more information visit:
www.TyrianPress.com
Email: info@TyrianPress.com
First printing, April 2017
Printed in U.S.A.

ISBN 978-0-9969024-1-0 paperback
ISBN 978-0-9969024-2-7 eBook
Library of Congress Control Number: 2017905081

Book Website
www.Iphelia.com
Email: info@Iphelia.com

In an effort to raise consciousness and heal the planet, Tyrian Press will donate a percentage of all book sales for the life of this book to the following organizations:

The Wellness Foundation
www.wellnessfound.org

Union of Concerned Scientists
www.ucsusa.org

ACKNOWLEDGMENTS

Thank you, Linsey D. D. Stevens, for putting your heart into this book. Your finely detailed editorial work and superb final suggestions set it free. Thank you, Tim Fox, for your thorough editorial work and helpful refining suggestions. Thank you, Mindy Carney, for your editorial work and for validating the importance and potency of this project. Thank you, Cora Allen, for your genius left-brain grounding of my right brain and balanced feedback and encouragement during those crucial organizing steps. Thank you, Jennifer Tompras, for believing in me and caring so deeply about this project and giving valuable editorial and design suggestions. You are a Lakshmi! Thank you, Amy D'Agrosa, for truly seeing and appreciating me and for teaching me about gratitude by what you radiate. I love you to infinity and beyond! Thank you, Jim Ross, for inspiring me through your own personal transformation, and for witnessing and supporting me in so many ways along the way. I love you, old friend. Thank you, Christine Mackey-Ross, for all your proofreading and feedback and for telling me, "This is your life's work, please spend the money and get a professional edit!" Thank you, Kristen Scheidter for your third-eye-wide proofreading and seeing so many things no one else saw! Thank you, Deb England, for your early editorial suggestions and encouragement. Thank you, Ildalucia Garza, for all your encouragement and invaluable artistic feedback on the initial impact of the imagery. Thank you, Marlene Littleton, for seeing and believing in me and this project and being a true friend from the day you came into my life. I love you.

I especially want to thank all of my clients and students. Thank you for all that you have shared with me and for all of your hard work. You are my greatest teachers. We made this together. It is for you. PTI tribes: Breath of Life, Dene-Tha, Detente, and Nuovo Cielo. You are the first in the procession of this march. Thank you for trusting me—you are all dragons!

To my teachers, David Hartman and Diane Zimberoff at the Wellness Institute in Issaquah, Washington, thank you for the tremendous gift you have given the world and for, "teaching the teachers and healing the healers." Thank to all my teachers and colleagues at the Wellness Institute including Susan Estep, Michael Malone, and Kathy Barringer. I have immense gratitude for the space you held for me over the years. I will pay it forward a thousand-fold. A special thanks to all the Wellness Tribes I have journeyed with along the way: Circle of Ancients, Gathering of the Clans, and Undefended Hearts. Many of the truths in this book were distilled through the work we did together.

A very deep and heartfelt thanks to my co-teacher and most trusted friend and ally Barbara Magallanes, for all your enthusiastic praise and encouragement—and for sitting beside me and being safe and true. Thank you for seeing me, B! I love you. We have much work to do!

Most of all I thank you, Jennifer Ann Stanley, my little wing, greatest supporter, personal cheerleader, playmate, fellow nerd, spiritual growth partner, and mother of my child. None of this is possible without you. You have given me the most. I love you all ways.

And finally, everyone, and there are many, whom I've ever disappointed, hurt, or betrayed, and everyone who has ever disappointed, hurt, or betrayed me: our shared pain has driven me to complete this work.

Read this book any way you want. Front to back, back to front, pick a page and go.

I suggest starting at the beginning. All of the content builds on the preceding material. My hope is that, as it builds, you find yourself ascending crescendos of insight and inspiration. As you read the story, take time to look at the pictures. "A picture is worth a thousand words." Try to connect with the images of the feelings. See if you can feel the feelings. Empathize with the characters. Notice what pictures you are more drawn to or disinterested in or even repulsed by. Observe your internal process as you go. Insights may come. Memories of personal experiences may come. Feelings may come. The story is a journey through the realm of feelings. It is a hero's journey. It is a story about us all.

There are two basic sections to this book: the graphic story and the inspirational teaching. Throughout the teaching portion there are images and parentheticals that reference parts of the graphic story. Toward the latter half of the book there is more reference material including *Feeling Awareness, A New Paradigm*, which is a list of 33 maxims derived from the content of the book, the *Empathy Knows Glossary* of feelings, and the *Appendix*, which includes a glossary of terms. The glossary of terms includes (1) clinical terms that might not be known to the layperson, (2) further exposition on some basic concepts that are used frequently throughout the text, and (3) a few simple terms like *validation* and *sympathy*, which during the editing process we decided would benefit from additional clarification. If while you are reading you find yourself wondering what something in italics means, the answer will very likely be found in the glossary of terms. All of the terms in the glossary include page references for the whole book.

There are portions of the text which contain practical instructions for achieving some desired end. All of these areas are listed as Practices in the table of contents but are not titled that way in the body of the text. This was a deliberate choice. The instructions are contemplative. It was thought that even without performing the tasks, simply reading through the exercises would stimulate feelings and generate insight. Therefore, titling those portions of the text as Practices seemed limiting and potentially misleading.

This book contains the most important things I believe I know for sure to be true. It is a creatively packaged amalgamation of all the things I've heard myself saying to myself over the years—as I appeared to be counseling and teaching my students. I feel it has been tremendously helpful for me to make this book. I hope you feel it's helpful to you. So much time and attention and energy has gone into creating it. Thank you for giving it *yours*.

CONTENTS

CONTENTS

CONTENTS

May this purple dragon heart,
Fly far true blazingly,
May it touch each inner child,
Help them stand and see.

If we feel our fear, our hurt and sadness,
Rage a graceful way,
We can know integral balanced power,
Upon the coming day.

When we care and clean and clear,
Reset our inner stage,
Love and joy and peace rain down,
Ripen mature age.

May all the children sing out loud,
May praises be the sound!
In the East, the North, the West and South,
Let Mother Earth be proud.

May we feel our Mother breathing easy,
Her children are awake!
And Father Sky watching over,
All we have at stake.

May we finally learn to live in love,
As all that we can be.
Our torn hearts mend enlarged,
Sprouting wings to set us free.

For Diya and Ovya,
Pieces of my heart,
Your insatiable joy colors these pages.

And for my son Sage,
And all the sensitive children of tomorrow.
May all awaken. May all rejoice.

*"The infinite wonders of the universe
are revealed to us in exact measure
as we are capable of receiving them.
The keenness of our vision
depends not on how much we can see,
but on how much we feel."*

–Helen Keller

We are all born with the capacity for empathy, but because adults have learned to refrain from expressing what they are really feeling, the practice is denied and the ability invalidated. Children are often systematically conditioned to ignore their own feelings and gradually lose the ability to empathize. This results in a cycle of emotional suppression which is passed on from generation to generation. One of the most powerful things we can do to break the cycle is to help children develop and retain their capacity for empathy, self-awareness, and creativity by teaching them the language of feelings.

Feeling words are more than labels; they are concepts that identify conditions in consciousness. The practice of identifying what one is feeling opens up another dimension of experience. This dimension of feelings precedes the physical dimension of the reality we live in. Feelings cause actions. They even create diseases and generate healings. Dispirited feelings narrow insight and blind possibility. Inspired feelings open doors to new endeavors and new inventions. All material motion ultimately begins as e-motion.

Most of the struggles we have in our relationships stem from an inability to be aware of our own feelings and the feelings of others, and to communicate on a level of feeling. Conflict is always about feeling and meaning, which are overlooked. We fight to be understood. We fight because we hurt. Resolution is always about paying attention to feeling and meaning. We share our feelings and empathize with others. We listen. We learn. We feel. We understand. We connect.

Teaching ourselves and our children to know and understand the power of feelings is the beginning of a more mature world. It is the beginning of a responsible world where human beings create consciously. It is the beginning of a more beautiful world in which our ever-expanding diversity is celebrated and universal love, respect, and consideration abound.

Thank you for sharing in this journey toward an awakened world.

1. Feelings are real.

2. Feelings are everywhere.

3. Feelings are messages from the self and others.

4. Feelings tell us who we are and what we prefer.

5. Feelings tell us what we are really being and what our real intentions are.

6. Feelings give us valuable information about everything we place our attention on.

7. Feeling words are symbols that describe conditions in consciousness.

8. Feeling words help us to stay conscious and help us communicate our experience.

• • •

Act I

The Awakening

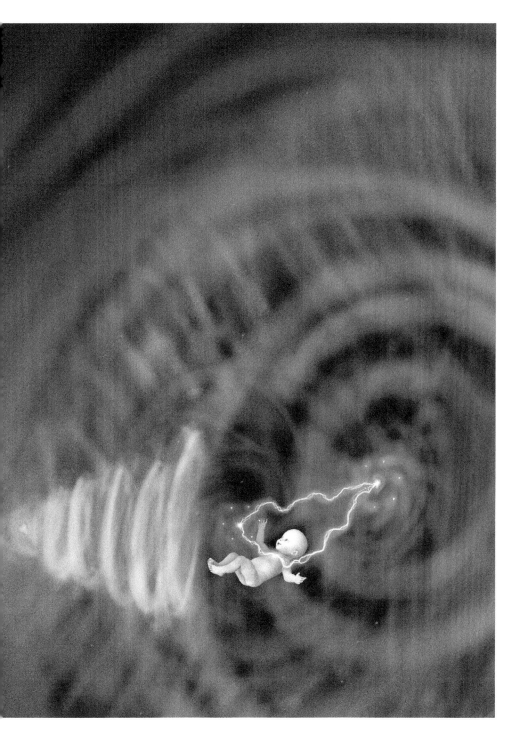

Iphelia was born with a special gift.

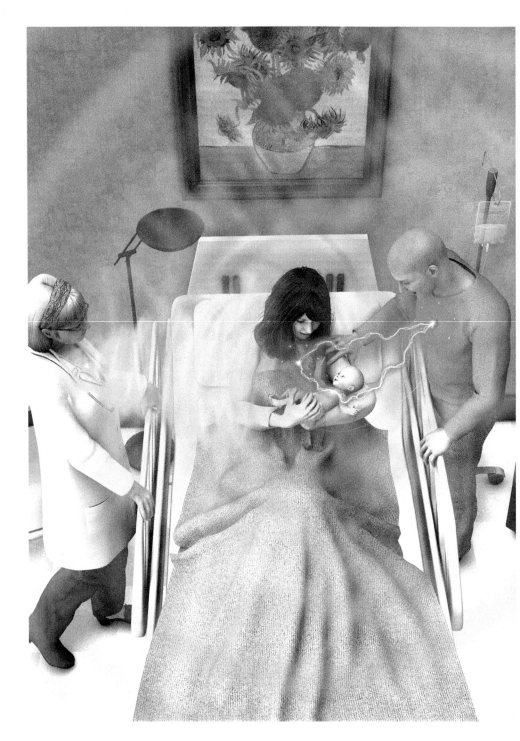

She could feel what others were feeling.

As a baby, she felt mostly Amused.

But as she grew older,

10

She became very Confused...

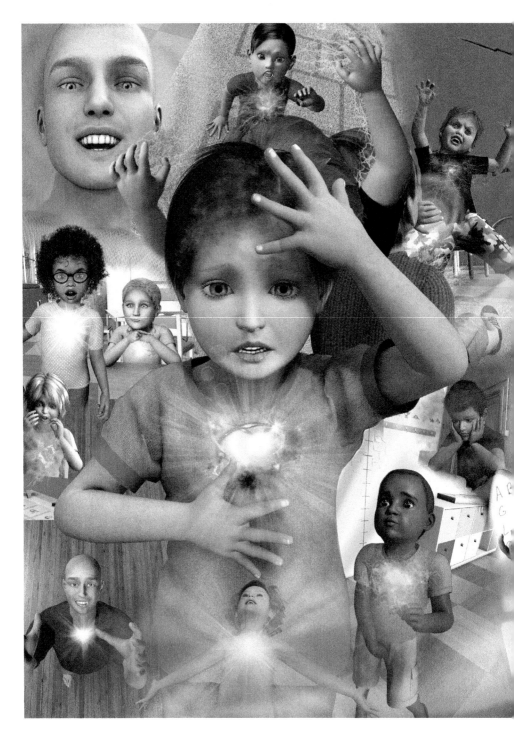

She would feel and feel and feel...

But she didn't understand why, and she wasn't sure it was real.

Sometimes what she felt...

Was totally fun!

But sometimes she couldn't wait...

For the feelings to be done.

17

Iphelia liked to draw pictures of everything she saw.

18

She even drew feelings and Mom would hang them on the wall.

19

Sometimes what others felt was different than what they would show...

But her mother said to trust her heart, and Iphelia continued to grow.

She soon learned words to describe all the things she could feel.

She grew more aware and her world became more real.

"If you want to find the secrets of the universe, think in terms of energy, frequency, and vibration."

—Nikola Tesla

Feelings Are Everywhere

t birth, we experience shock. When we take our first breath, we are completely disoriented by our newly acquired five senses, grappling to manage them while assimilating into the physical world. After the physical senses are understood, other subtle or intuitive senses have a chance to develop.

Imagine we have an emotional body that gives us feedback much like the feedback the senses of our physical bodies have given us since birth. As children, we used our five senses to learn about three-dimensional reality. We learned that fire is hot, gravity pulls down, how to walk, talk, listen, and judge distance. As all that was happening, our senses relayed some kind of vibrational contrast to our brains. There was light and darkness, silence and sound, scent, stench, sweet, sour, slathers of form and texture, and the absence of it all. Ultimately we sensed pain in contrast with other sensations and then mostly chose to do what we perceived as less painful. This is how we came to survive and thrive in the material world. We learned from our pain and eventually formed a functional frame, which empowered us to navigate physical space.

As we grow older, we develop into more psychologically and spiritually sophisticated beings. Our perception of reality is less physical, and our range of experience becomes more metaphysical. In fact, what we discover is that our reality is quite mutable and is filled with mental and emotional patterns that we have created or adopted from those around us.

Children who are naturally sensitive, and children who have not been conditioned to ignore or repress their feelings, may be more affected by subtle interactions in larger groups. They may have a harder time in school, seem withdrawn, or appear to learn more slowly. This happens because they are processing more information. Iphelia was initially overwhelmed by all the feelings she was sensing and confused by them. She was especially challenged when her father's facial expression was not congruent with what she was feeling from him (p. 20). This is a common way in which feelings are invalidated or contradicted by the adults in a child's life. A parent's own emotional repression or inauthenticity can be an experiential deception that gradually calls into question a child's inner guidance and intuition. "What's wrong, Daddy?" "Nothing's wrong, sweetheart. Daddy's fine," seems harmless and even protective from a "sensible" perspective. But from a process perspective, these simple remarks can plant a seed of confusion, casting doubt on the child's experience of her natural emotional sensitivity.

Feelings are everywhere. They are all around us and inside of us. So it is incredibly important to pay attention to, and *validate*, the feelings of our children. Our emotions are both the sensors and the creators of our subjective world. Just as our physical senses interpret vibration to help us sense the material world, our emotions are the experience of vibration from whatever we fix our attention to. Emotions give us a sense of contrast between what we are being and what we are perceiving. And they tell us how we are subjectively vibrating in contrast with how we want to be vibrating. They tell us what and who we like and don't like, and they tell us when and how we like ourselves. From childhood on, our feelings are the guiding lights to who we truly want to become. They are the voice of our conscience.

Act II

The Lessons

Iphelia learned Happy...

and Glad.

29

She learned Frustrated...

and Mad.

31

She learned Hurt...

and Sad.

33

She learned Startled...

34

and Afraid.

35

She learned Peaceful...

Calm...

Secure...

38

and Safe.

She learned Nervous...

40

Guilty…

41

and Ashamed.

She learned Pure...

43

Innocent...

and even Blame.

She learned Tired...

46

Disappointed...

Depressed...

and Bored.

She learned Confident...

Assertive...

And Self-Assured.

53

She learned Embarrassed...

Abandoned...

Lonely...

and Desperate.

She learned Worry…

58

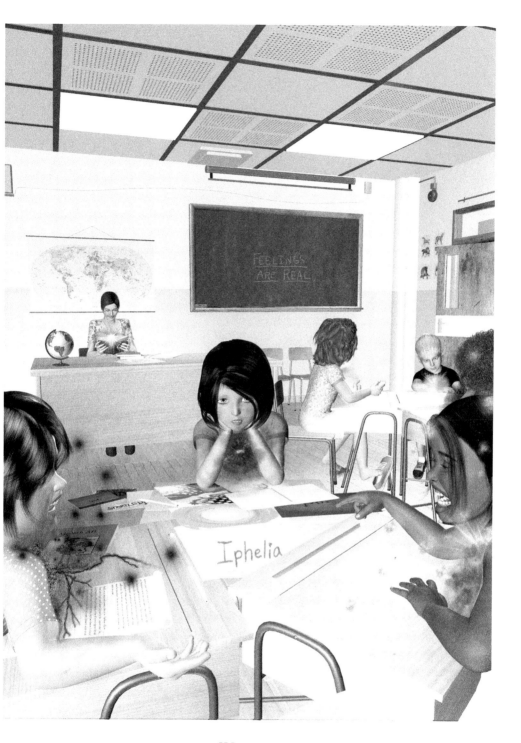

Weary...

59

and Repressed Resentment.

She learned Angry...

61

Weak...

and Strong.

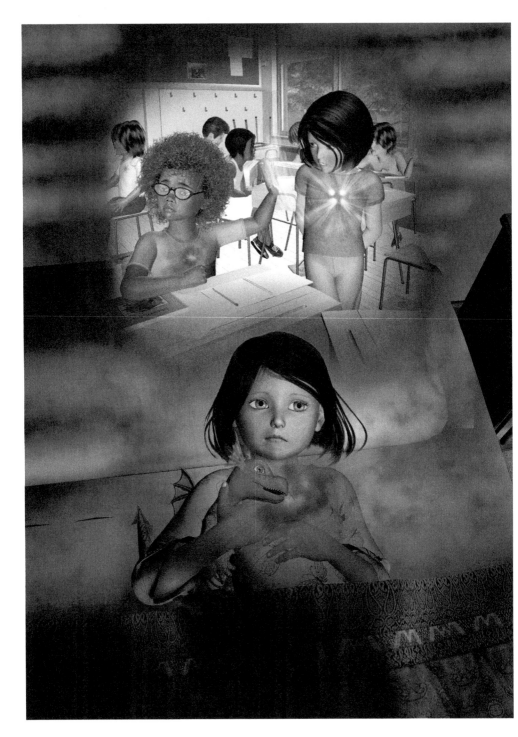

She learned Doubtful...

Hopeful...

Right...

and Wrong.

67

She learned she could feel different feelings at the same time...

But there was always one feeling at the front of her mind.

*"There is only one disease—congestion,
and one cure—circulation."*

–Florence Scovel Shinn

Feelings Are Messages

here is great relief when we allow ourselves to release feeling-energy from our bodies. Sometimes this energy arises immediately in response to new experience, sometimes it builds up over time due to suppression or avoidance, and sometimes it is a freeing of energy that was once repressed because of our inability to process certain, often painful, experiences at an earlier stage of development. Allowing emotion to take motion allows for change. Our perceptions of ourselves, our world, and the challenges we face all change when our energy moves. The way others perceive us changes when they witness this energy move within us. Even the way others unconsciously respond to us changes when we allow our emotional body's old, congested energy to move. When a grudge is held, the grudge is felt and responded to, even if it isn't consciously acknowledged by anyone involved. When sadness or grief are not allowed release, the pain stays and haunts the feeler for life. When healthy anger is not expressed, we feel powerless and eventually become depressed. The volcano of our own expanding worth and self-respect is never allowed to erupt, and we miss all the great realizations that would naturally bubble up.

When Iphelia finally allows herself the release of her anger, she tears her room and drawings apart and a great surge of power runs through her body. After the storm calms, she feels empowered and begins making healthier choices. She grieves the loss of her friendship with Olivia, allowing herself to feel her sadness (weak, p. 62). She goes back to drawing because that is what she loves to do, and rather than pining for approval, she begins to set boundaries with the kids who have made fun of her (strong, p. 63). She ponders how she can repair her relationship with Olivia (doubtful and hopeful, p. 64-65), and even begins to reflect on her behavior and how she has felt about it (right and wrong, p. 66-67). Ultimately, her awareness deepens and she knows this is because she has listened for and received the messages of her feelings. Had she not allowed herself the explosion of anger, she would not have let go of trying so hard to prove herself to every-one. And she could never have come to the series of soul-freeing realiza-tions that follow.

All about. Feelings
By Iphelia

1. Feelings are messages

2. I have to finish my feelings to Get the Message !

3. Feelings not finished stay.

4. Not finished feelings make me tired

5. More not finished feelings make us mean

6. Finished feelings make us Smart, strong, happy, nice.

Act III

The Gift

Then one night when she was all alone,

74

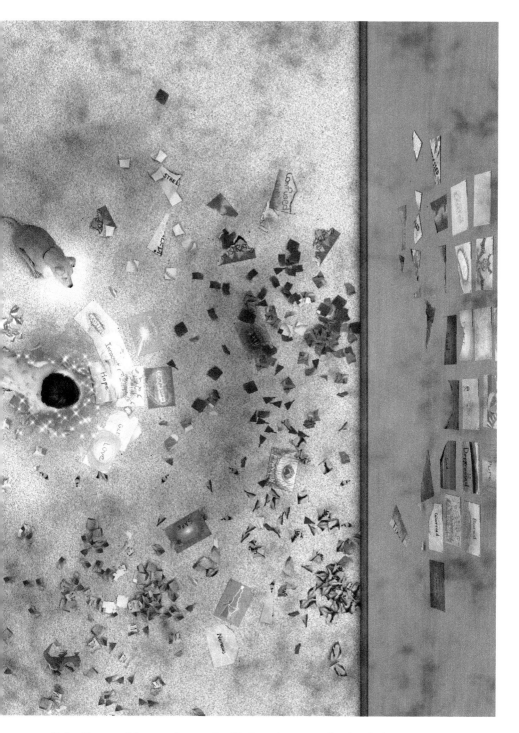

Iphelia would sort through all the pictures she had thrown.

75

She picked out her most favorite feelings of all...
She decided these were the pictures she would hang on the wall.

She hung Joy and Love and Peace and Free.

She hung Innocent and Grateful and Compassion and Glee.

Then in her mind came a light for her to see!
She could be any way, any time she wants to be!

"I can be any way, any time I want to be!
I am grateful, I am happy, I am proud, I am free!
I am love, I am joy, I am glee! I am glee! I am glee!"

Then she said it out loud again, but this time feeling each word to the end.

"I can be any way, any time I want to be!
I am grateful, I am happy, I am proud, I am free!
I am love, I am joy, I am GLEE-GLEE-GLEE!"

Iphelia then began to shout!
...which left no room for hurt, sadness, fear, or even doubt.

Iphelia was jumping, dancing and singing her song...
When she suddenly stopped and remembered feeling wrong.

82

She thought of Olivia and how she felt her feel.
She wanted to share her song and give Olivia new zeal.

So she imagined a plan to make Olivia aware.
She wrote down words and made copies she would share.

She would wait until recess when everyone was away.
And talk with Olivia about starting a new day.

85

She would tell her she had choice to feel big or small.
We always have choice, there is never a wall.

And when Olivia was ready, she stopped her mope, and Iphelia could see she was ready for hope! Then Iphelia showed her the words of her song...

...And hopeful Oliva began reading along. They read the words out loud again and again. They chanted with rhythm, feeling each word ascend!

"I can be any way, any time I want to be!
I am grateful, I am happy, I am proud, I am free!
I am love, I am joy, I am GLEE-GLEE-GLEE!"

Soon Olivia was smiling and really feeling great.
And soon there was not just two singing, but four, then six, then eight!

89

Then all the kids on the playground gathered around...

And sang Iphelia's song. It was the most beautiful sound!

"I can be any way, any time I want to be!
I am grateful, I am happy, I am proud, I am free!
I am love, I am joy, I am GLEE-GLEE-GLEE!"

"I can be any way, any time I want to be!
I am grateful, I am happy, I am proud, I am free!
I am love, I am joy, I am GLEE-GLEE-GLEE!"

"I can be any way, any time I want to be!
I am grateful, I am happy, I am proud, I am free!
I am love, I am joy, I am GLEE-GLEE-GLEE!"

And when recess was over and the children went inside...

It was a happy day for everyone—smiles were very wide.

And later that evening before Iphelia went to bed,
she drew new favorite feelings that came to her head...

She drew Caring and Sharing and Generous and Kind.

And as her mother left the room she felt a Grateful peace of mind.

Then later that night while Iphelia slept,
she felt the most incredible feelings as she dreamt.

101

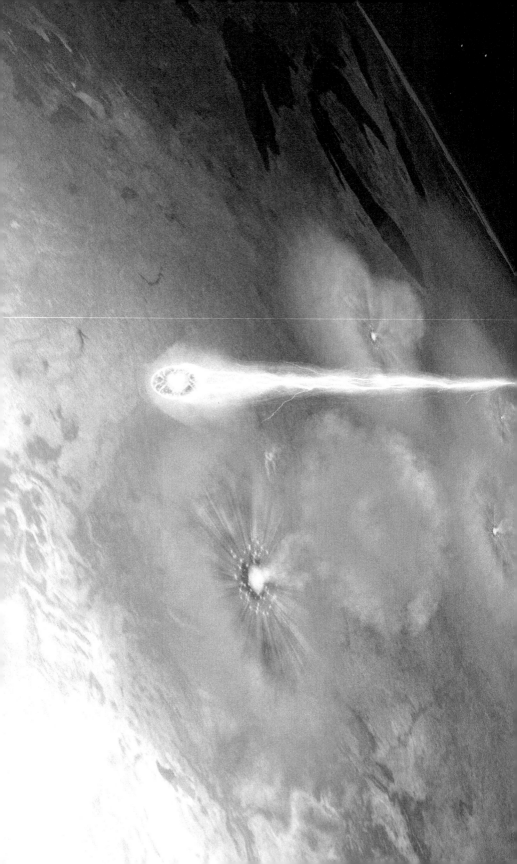

"The best and most beautiful things in the world cannot be seen or even touched. They must be felt within the heart."

–Helen Keller

Feelings are Real

eelings are real. Feelings are everywhere. We may not see them, but they are always happening. They happen within us. They happen around us. They happen between us. Before anyone does anything in the world, there is feeling. As everything happens in the world, there is feeling. Conscious acknowledgement of our experience of feeling is essential to finding meaning in our lives and in relationship with ourselves and each other. Moving through life without examining our feelings leaves a void in our experience. It hobbles our ability to know ourselves and connect with others. Without feelings we are blind and clumsy. Without feelings there cannot be empathy. Consequences for the repression of our feelings range from personal dissatisfaction in life and relationships to the pandemic of short-sightedness, which is generating increasing tragedy on a global scale. Genocide, terrorism, torture, slavery, sex trafficking, female genital mutilation, racism, hate, animal abuse, all forms of oppression, all inequities— first-world robbing third-world resources, poverty, hunger, ignorance, and disease all extend from our collective emotional repression.

An insensitive father who was raised to deny his own feelings denies his son the need for praise and affirmation. His son grows callous and compensates for worthlessness by ruthlessly seeking to build a financial empire which takes advantage of its employees, its consumers, and the earth. Another father's suppressed grief perpetuates a longing for vengeance that is transmitted and instilled into his children as justified hate and discrimination.

A mother who learned to deny her feelings of worthiness and power toler-ates the abuse of her emotionally wounded husband and transmits shame and guilt to her children. Those children grow up to live lives of fear and subservience. Another mother leaves the abuse but also leaves her trust as she overly controls and emotionally abuses her children who grow up cal-lous and incapable of trust and intimacy.

The scenarios are infinite but the result is the same for all of us. How we relate to each other today is the amalgamation of legacies of undigested feel-ing. As children, the experiences seem small and their impact fleeting. But over time our defense mechanisms evolve into more intensified versions of their original forms. Left unaddressed, those old wounded parts embed into our personalities as we make ever more detrimental choices for ourselves and the world around us. If we are going to survive, we have to wake up to how we have been affected by what *has been* and consciously choose what we are going *to be*. At this time in history, paying attention to and exploring the dimension of feelings is vitally important. Let us begin…

The images in this book illustrate an individual view of a universal phenomenon. The subjective experience and growth of any individual will determine an alternate visualization of any particular feeling. In this way the images are indeed meant to be understood as examples of actual perceptions of real phenomena. Everyone's experience will vary to differing degrees. One person's experience of sadness might feel and look quite different from another's, but there will also be invariable similarities. Universal archetypes and the contrasting reference of line, shape, form, intensity, space, color, and texture will always illustrate that our consciousness is connected.

The practice of *free association*, or observing whatever images passively emerge in the mind when it is focused on a particular feeling, can reveal much. When we visualize feelings in this way, we bring greater awareness to the quality of our experience at any given moment. In a sense, we make the unseen *seen* and with this added information are better able to make wise and healthy decisions for ourselves, our communities, and the world. This is not an unnatural process. It is quite natural. We have only forgotten.

Intention Setting (IS)

Before beginning any introspective process, setting an intention is very helpful. When we set an intention, we declare what something IS. We give trajectory to the action about to be taken. The mind is focused on an intended outcome. We are letting the subconscious part of ourselves know what to do.

Saying intentions out loud works on various levels. It activates the body—we breathe, move our mouths, our tongues, maybe even our shoulders, arms, and hands. It activates parts of the brain that would otherwise not move. We hear ourselves. We declare our intention out loud, making it stronger and dominant over the already-present chatter circulating in our mind and body. In short, when we say the intention out loud, we are making it a part of us. We inhale, exhale, vibrate, and become.

Saying intentions out loud also gives us an opportunity to notice any resistance to our chosen statement. When setting intentions, feelings of anxiety, fear, anger, or judgment about the statements can be an indicator of unconscious *resistance*. Resistance usually indicates that on some level, we feel fear. The feeling of fear likely means we may soon become aware of something that some part of us does not want to see. Just notice this feeling and lean into it. Set the intention anyway. There is great awareness and knowledge on the other side.

Seeing Feelings (SEER)

Set your intention. Say out loud three times, "**I pay attention to myself**," "**I really want to know myself**," "**I want to know what I am feeling**."

1. **Slow.** Slow down and begin by being present with your body. Be aware of your posture and position. Allow your mental attention to encompass your body, tracing its surface. See if you can focus all of your senses on your body. Notice your breath and beating heart.

2. **Express.** Allow the feeling or feelings to move. Let the body move with them. Give the feelings words. What are they saying? What are they doing?

3. **Envision.** Visualize what you are feeling. Envision the form and texture and color. Envision the movement of the feeling.

4. **Record.** With colored pencils, crayons, or paint, draw it out. Make it visible. Notice what other thoughts, insights, and realizations emerge as you draw your feelings. Write them down.

The visualization of our feelings is a window's view of the truth. A view of our interdependence. A view to what we are really doing and being. Visualizing feelings gives us a window's view of our abuse, our sacrifice, of our selfish and our selfless. When we learn to allow and observe them, our feelings always tell us what is really happening. Our feelings can even tell us who we really are, and that is everything.

Discovering who we really are is the most valuable lesson attending to our feelings has to offer. There are no shortcuts. Deceptions are mere temporary congestions of the inevitable. A lie is only a delay. Nothing is hidden. All is accounted for. All has effect. Our emotional shadows follow us wherever we go. When this truth is fully understood, our relationships with everything change. We can't help but begin striving to be honest and authentic to ourselves and the world. If we lie in a relationship, our experience of the relationship is puppeted and without trust. If we hide our true feelings, we never feel connected or loved, and we ever-weaken our ability to love. Conversely, when we strive to be true to the people we love in our lives, we build magnificent bridges of light upon which great shipments of love and affirmation can be transported. Then a miracle is possible. Here's the miracle:

We realize the most beautiful version,
we can conceive ourselves,
and our fellow humans,
as being.

Realizing this kind of beauty is discovering who we truly are. Empathy is the key to this realization. Empathy toward the self and others opens us up to the reality we long for. We realize the trust, the connection, the love, the beauty—knowing who we truly are and truly seeing one another—all perceived through feeling. A miracle, only possible through feeling.

But coming to this realization is not one simple "Aha" moment. We have to evolve. We have to become something new and different. For each of us, this emotional evolution is a very personal and mythic journey. And like any good hero's journey, there are challenges along the way.

"We always see our own unavowed mistakes in our opponent."

–Carl Jung

The Wounded Empath

he experience of empathy is often distorted by the subjective struggles of the feeler. Naturally occurring remnants of childhood trauma or abuse, in any measure, cause suffering in the form of deep-seated shame or inferiority. We each find a way to live with our wounds. For those of us who manage to find power, we may tend to compensate for feelings of inferiority and insecurity by positioning ourselves as superior in our awareness of others. The wounded empath says, "I know better what you are feeling and experiencing than you do." Ultimately, this becomes hurtful to both ourselves and others around us. The capacity to empathize becomes an instrument to more effectively control others. Trust and safety are never realized and real connection is never established.

Those of us who feel less empowered may struggle with establishing healthy boundaries. This can manifest as unhealthy isolation or extreme codependency. We may tend to isolate, by hiding or pushing people away, to create some semblance of safety. Or the capacity to empathize is used to fuse to another person and become completely absorbed in his or her experience to find safety. In other words, "If I pay complete attention to how you feel and take care of your feelings, then you'll love me and I'll be okay." The powerless empath never learns to connect with the self and eventually feels abandoned or abused by the person they have chosen to identify with. Real connection is never established.

These two general ways of dealing with the wounded self represent two sides of a functional polarity. One wars with the world and the other overextends to the world. One attempts to take up space and assert control over the environment. The other attempts to stay out of the way and/or give away space—disappear from the environment. Left unchecked, these defense mechanisms of hyper-assertion and hyper-passivity evolve into unique forms of *narcissism* and *codependency*.

In its purity, our narcissistic self is completely self-absorbed and has little consideration or care for the experience of others except for how we might benefit and continue to feed the drive to compensate for inferiority. It is only a matter of time before this self-centered bubble pops. Isolation increases and the capacity for awareness of others decreases until we can no longer keep the facade alive. Eventually we are abandoned by every real connection we've ever had, and we live alone in an ivory tower regaling the ego with exaggerated tales of greatness from our past or delusional fantasies of the future.

Concurrently, our codependent self appears to be completely focused on the needs of others, but this is really a veiled attempt to establish control by cultivating need or dependency in others. The codependent lives in fear of abandonment and compensates by working hard to be the hero and supplier of love for everyone around. Here, too, it is only a matter of time before the bubble pops. Anger builds as we resent the dependency we have created, or eventually we are persecuted by our dependents for the ways we have prevented them from becoming whole.

Either way or a unique combination of both, the empath splits the self and identifies with a polarity. But we need both sides of all of our selves. We need the ability to be assertive and passive, aggressive and sensitive, guarded and vulnerable. We need all our light and all our dark, all our strength and all our weakness. We are meant to be whole.

When the self is split, the result is always to see outside of the self the parts we have lost or driven away. Empathy is clouded by our confused state. We unconsciously keep making our way to the same or similar experience that we split from. And each time, for most of us, we split even further.

The Fog of Projection

As human beings, each of us is filled with personal emotional complexity which has the potential to really fog up our capacity for empathy. The biggest way empathy gets distorted is via the phenomenon of projection.

You spot it, you got it.
You see it, you be it.
You shun it, you done it.
Beauty is in the eye of the beholder.
And so is shit.

Projection is when we assume people are being how we imagine them to be. And more than that, we unconsciously attribute to them aspects of ourselves that we are in conflict with or simply don't want to acknowledge. Here's how it happens in a nutshell. We grow up absorbing the *contagion of separation* that exists all around us. We take on a lot of fear and judgment and try to adapt to the environment to secure love and acceptance. But this makes us feel more separate because we are not being ourselves. We feel separate from ourselves and from others, and we eventually learn to actually separate internally from parts of our own being. We internalize the fearful judgments of our parents, our friends, the culture, and the media, and pretty soon we feel a lot of confusion, so much that many of us spend

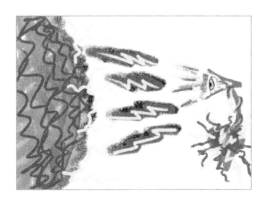

the rest of our lives feeling imprisoned by it. We become so conflicted inside that we begin projecting that conflict onto our world. Simply put, individuals with a lot of inner conflict perceive the world as a very conflicted place and find conflict with it. Individuals who have achieved some degree of self-acceptance perceive the world with acceptance and find harmony with it, even in the midst of conflict.

As we get older, our fragmented sense of self causes us all kinds of problems in the form of projections. We might judge or attack the reflection of something we don't want to acknowledge exists within ourselves. Like the homophobe, the racist, the bigot, and the bully, all of whom compensate for their own self-perceived inferiority by preying on what they see as weak or wrong in others. We might project our own guilt. Like the cheating husband accusing his faithful wife of flirting or the self-deprecating person always apologizing to others for nothing, projecting guilt for the ways he constantly abandons and betrays himself. We may also project to avoid parts of ourselves. Like the frustrated parent who focuses on the myriad of problems her child is having, without ever considering the source from whence those very behaviors were learned. Or the rescuing friend who focuses on caring for the wound of another in order to substitute caring for his own. Projection can even take the form of hero worship, praising an external authority in order to avoid responsibility or to escape knowledge of the much feared greatness within the self!

Projection is pervasive. Everybody does it. It happens all the time. It's not a curse. It's not a problem. It is not possible to stop, nor is it something we want to stop. Projection helps us get to know ourselves. Before we can become conscious of any new part of the self, we first experience it outside of ourselves by way of projection. This is especially evident in childhood, as we attribute god-like qualities to our parents.

Eventually, projection becomes a powerful defense mechanism, helping us suppress awareness we are not ready or wanting to assimilate. But as we grow and mature and the natural expansion of consciousness presses on, suppression becomes futile. Whatever we cover up within the self inevitably appears before us. Our mirrors are angels sent from heaven agreeing to play the roles we have yet to find the courage to see and accept as parts of ourselves. The mystery of life works incessantly, conspiring to show us what we do not yet see, which can ultimately set us free. Cooperating means that when we find what is missing in our brother, we choose to look for what is more in our self. The answer is always to look within.

The source of projection can always be traced back to a wound. But before that trace can be made and medicine applied, the wound must be identified. Bringing what is unconscious to consciousness is challenging, but necessary to clear the fog. When we are unconscious of our projections, they have us. It's like we are living in a crazy dream that everyone can see but us. We blame others for our discord and we give our power away. But when we acknowledge our projections, our perception of ourselves and our world deepens. We see more and can choose to be more. We stop complaining and find creative solutions to the challenges we face. We heal. We grow. We reclaim our power.

In the end, projection teaches us that all the characteristics we love and judge exist within the self. All judgment is self-judgment. If we are to achieve clean empathy, we must fully accept and embrace all of the self and in turn, all of the self of others.

Identifying Projections (5WME)

In recent history the five W questions have been used as a tool of focus for most forms of journalism, research, and investigation. Those questions are who, what, when, where, and why. In the case of identifying and understanding projections, the question is always *who* and the answer is always *me*.

With a little honesty and sincere effort we can become conscious of our projections. Take some deep breaths and quiet your mind. Set a clear intention to really get to know yourself better. Before you continue reading, say these affirmations out loud 3 times, **"I am humble," "I am profoundly honest with myself"** and **"I really want to know the truth."**

Then ask yourself these questions. Pay attention to feelings as you ask the questions.

1. Who really makes me mad? Who are the people whom I really dislike in my world? What about them really bothers me? The mirror may be exaggerated, but these are the parts of ourselves we don't like. If we have difficulty seeing how we relate to others in the way we dislike, we can then ask if we relate to ourselves in that way. Toward others or toward the self, one or both will most likely be true.

2. Who do I avoid interacting with? Who am I afraid of talking with or making eye contact with? What is going to happen if I do interact with them? What will they see? Or what do I not want to see when I see them? These may be parts of ourselves in need of healing. Parts we have not fully developed or incorporated into our daily living. Parts of ourselves we need to work on developing. Parts we have not yet received strength and wholeness from.

3. **Who am I always apologizing to? Do I apologize too much? What am I apologizing for, if anything?** The trespasses we perceive ourselves delivering to those we unnecessarily apologize to are very likely going to be analogous to trespasses we put upon ourselves.

4. **Whose ass am I kissing? Who do I praise too much? What do I really like about them?** These may be parts of ourselves we have not yet realized even exist or parts we are afraid to acknowledge. Oftentimes these are parts of ourselves we avoid being aware of for fear of what it would mean and the change it would bring.

5. **Who am I? Am I not this? Am I only that? Or am I more? Am I all of it? Who am I beyond my projections?** These questions precipitate further contemplation. Paradoxically, the answers are best understood through the continual excavation of all the limiting self-concepts we discover ourselves not to be. We can then begin reclaiming all the parts of ourselves we have pushed away via projection.

If you are having trouble identifying the parts of yourself your projections represent, try this: Imagine being the person you find yourself reacting to. Feel what it feels like to be them. Whatever you perceive them feeling, allow yourself to feel that. Then ask, "When in my life do I feel these same or similar feelings? When is this same or similar energy active within me?" Or in the case of those we feel inferior to, "Is this feeling in some way missing in my life? Is it a feeling I want to feel more of? When would this feeling be useful in my life?"

Still struggling? Feeling brave? After spending some time with the questions alone, find a good, honest, and trustworthy friend—someone you are close to—someone who really knows you. Read him or her the affirmations out loud 3 times. Let him or her know you want the truth. Then ask your friend the same questions about yourself.

Who who-who
who-who-who
Who

"We think we listen, but very rarely do we listen with real understanding, true empathy. Yet listening, of this very special kind, is one of the most potent forces for change that I know."

–Carl Rogers

The Healing'em Path to Clean Empathy

Real empathy is only possible when the feeler is on a personal path to healing. The *Healing Empath* seeks to understand the meaning of her experience and the experience of others with absolute patience and acceptance. The Healing Empath practices personal empathy, establishing a real connection with the self, thus becoming more capable of really connecting with others. She realizes her tendency to project. She knows that projecting an assumption is actually a fear-driven act, which ultimately serves the purpose of avoidance. She accepts that whatever she is perceiving to cause emotional discord in her outer life has only been allowed entry through the compromise of her own subjective boundaries; or by the old wounded parts of herself affecting the condition of her relationship with her *true self*. She has realized that resolution lies within. She is on a path to healing all the parts of herself that hold her back. There is no more room for blame. The Healing Empath knows she is the one who is completely responsible for her experience.

Accepting responsibility for the self is empowering and freeing. It releases our friends and family from the silent burden of blame. It releases them from expectation. We don't need others to be any certain way so that we can feel the way we want or be who we want to be. And when we free ourselves to be ourselves, we effortlessly support others in doing the same. We detach from will or want about anyone else's choices because we have a larger deeper need for them to make their own choices. We want them to learn from their own lives and we want their learning to be theirs. We want them to have ownership of themselves and feel completely self-determined. We have come to a point where we can allow others to make their own mistakes because we so fully appreciate what we have learned from our own. We become Healing Empaths on the Healing'em Path, healing all our parts first, so we can really show up and be a healing presence providing *Clean Empathy* for our friends, our families, and our communities.

Clean Empathy

Clean empathy perceives accurately because it is not clouded by projection. Clean empathy is received gracefully because it is not forced. Clean empathy allows. It is compassionate and patient. It sees. People feel seen and understood by clean empathy. It soothes suffering, and by its witness offers safety, which invites the healthy release of what is congested or repressed. Since *compassion* and goodwill toward all beings are the natural impulses of the open heart, clean empathy does not judge or project assumptions, or tell another person what they are feeling. Clean empathy knows that assuming to wholly know the experience of another is counterproductive to anything beneficial or healing. Clean empathy supports others in identifying their own feelings and coming to their own insights.

Personal Empathy

The key to achieving clean empathy for another is developing *Personal Empathy* for the self. Real connection can only happen when a person is connected with their true self. Empathy toward the self is necessary to establish a connection with the true self. Personal empathy is discovering and maintaining a genuine caring relationship toward the self. To care about the self means paying attention to our feelings and paying attention to the quality of the feelings that different experiences, behaviors, and thoughts generate. And then choosing to make choices inside and outside toward what is going to lead us to a better-feeling place.

In addition to paying attention to feelings, personal empathy means practicing expressing positive feelings toward the self. It means looking in the mirror, putting your hand on your heart, and striving to really like what you're seeing and feeling. The conversation we have with the self is always being had through feelings. Having a relationship with one's self means being committed to staying conscious of this dialogue of feelings that is happening all the time. Only after healthy personal empathy is established can we clearly differentiate what is subjective experience and what is the experience of another, outside of ourselves. Personal empathy is the path of the healing empath; without it, clean empathy is not possible.

"What is to give light, must endure burning."

–Victor Frankl

Core Feelings

eveloping personal empathy requires a commitment to allowing the *natural cycle of emotion* to ensue. We have to *feel* our feelings to get their messages and really get to know ourselves. A more in-depth contemplation of core feelings will be helpful in working toward this aim.

Anger

Most of the time, anger arises as a secondary feeling, ensuring repression of the more vulnerable feeling beneath the surface. Feelings like fear, hurt, or sadness begin to rise, and we immediately, sometimes instantly, conjure some degree of emotional intensity, or anger, instead of allowing the core feeling to express and move.

This is not to say that *Secondary Anger* does not have its place or usefulness. It can be useful or even required for our survival. But there is a difference between shouting at our children to shock them out of running into the street, and shouting to prevent them from spilling milk. Let them spill the milk. And experience the natural consequence of not paying attention to what is around them by cleaning up the mess, even if you have to help. Then they will learn and internalize the lesson. And later they will watch where they are running without relying on shocking direction.

But why do we sometimes not have the patience to allow for spilt milk? Our anger is not about the child or the milk. It is about us.

Why is it I don't have time? When did I decide I needed to be in a hurry? Or when did I conclude that it was a punishable offense to spill milk? Heaven is in the other direction. A direction of introspection and self-healing. Not projection and blame. There are innumerable examples of how we project our neuroses and attempt to suppress vulnerable feelings with force and anger. But healing will always mean becoming conscious of our limited construct and of the childhood-fear-ridden conclusion that created it. Then we can choose a new conclusion and create a new construct, or set of beliefs and behaviors, for healing. In this case, healing a hurried and perfectionist lifestyle.

Secondary Anger is what's left of our old lizard brain's fight or flight response. It's primitive. Think dinosaur age. It functions automatically, like a machine. But as humans, we often have this kind of reaction to something much less scary than a Tyrannosaurus rex about to eat us. The reaction is most likely about some experience of powerlessness we had as a child. This is why we must practice staying conscious of what we are feeling, so the old defense machine isn't automatically taking over and cutting us off from connection, healing, or a real solution to the problem.

The *Healthy Release of Anger* is a lightning storm in the night. It wakes us up to what is on the horizon and welcomes the rain of feelings previously repressed. The healthy release of anger restores balance and is most often released in private. Rather than project onto others, we might hit a pillow, scream while we are in the car, or channel the energy into physical exercise. When we fully allow expression of this anger in a healthy way, we often spontaneously recall a traumatic experience that left us feeling powerless. There might be a flash of the childhood incident that scared us into hurrying, or perhaps a rapid tour of the series of events instilling the need to be perfect. We become conscious of the source of repressed feeling and instinctively push back. As these powerful feelings pass over the nervous system, a balance is restored. We finally give ourselves permission to slow down and make mistakes. And paradoxically, we may become more timely and precise than ever before, but without all the once-fearful and anxiety-ridden effort.

Conscious Anger is rare. It is intentional. The feeler chooses to feel and express the anger but is not possessed by it. It is not reactive. It is mature and responsive. It comes from care. It is the expression of a controlled measure of intensity, which serves the purpose of keeping healthy boundaries in relationships and maintaining an energetic balance within the self. It rises up to meet confrontation with just the right amount of firmness and ferocity. In challenging situations it says, "This is where I draw the line," and "This is how I will respond to your behavior if you continue," and "I mean it!" When used to set boundaries in relationships, conscious anger counterweights the movement of its opposing force. It mirrors the energy it faces, and it rises and falls as quickly or as slowly as needed. Once the confrontation is over and the boundary is effectively set or maintained, the intensity drops and feelings of harmony and cooperation resume.

As we develop and mature, conscious anger can be expressed as a teaching response to assist in restoring balance outside of the self. Ultimately, this is still connected to the self, but in a more intentional and altruistic way. The individual is consciously building the self and using emotional intensity to establish a larger beneficent presence in the outer world. Examples of this might be protesting inequality, or standing up for someone who is being bullied or shamed. The expression of conscious anger dissipates as quickly as it rises and is forgotten. No grudges are held. Balance is restored inside and out.

Anger Release Ritual (ARR)

The healthy release of anger is decongesting. It allows us to finally get with all the feelings that have been repressed. It also restores balance in the nervous system. Anger's power can easily awaken us from a slumber of depression or passivity. When we feel our anger and put it where it belongs, our world view changes. We walk tall as we were meant to walk. We talk strong as we were meant to talk. We empower ourselves to breathe fully and express fully. Here's what you'll need: a sturdy wiffle ball bat, a large cardboard box, some duct tape, and one big fat marker.

Set a clear intention to really allow yourself to feel your anger. Say these affirmations out loud three times, **"I have anger," "I allow myself to feel my anger," "I have power," "I allow myself to feel my power."** Give yourself permission to really lose your shit!

1. **Allow some time and space** for yourself to explore all the ways you feel angry. Find a place where you can be alone to make a lot of noise. Make a list. Or, if you feel the anger but don't really know what it's about, that's fine, too. You can still draw it. If you are a person who has a hard time getting in touch with anger, the list may look more like all the things you are afraid of or worry about. After you finish your list, give it form. Build your box. Tape it shut. Draw and write all over the box. Give each topic its proportional representation of space on the box. If there's a lot of anger or fear, give it a lot of space. Some topics may require their own box. As you create your box allow yourself to be fully aware of the feelings you have about each topic. Feel as though you are infusing the box with the objects of your anger. Place the box before you. Lay the wiffle ball bat directly in front of you, between you and the box. Now stare at your box. Breathe deeply. See if you can feel all the ways your box is holding you back.

2. **Release your rage!** When you are ready, pick up the bat and have a go at it. Hit the box as hard as you can. Use your words. Say out loud exactly what you are thinking when you hit. This is a proclamation. Proclaim your power. Speak your truth to your oppressors! Each person, any groups or organizations, Uncle Sam, or any part of your self that feels out of your control. Put it where it goes! Whatever comes. Name them and tell them, "No more!" "Never again!" "You can't hurt me anymore!" "I decide!" "I choose!" "Stay away from me!" "Get out!" "Go away!" "I'm done!" "It's over!" Profanity is welcome here. Don't hold back. Saying exactly what you mean generates insight and rewires the old patterns in a specific way. You might be surprised by what comes out of your mouth once you truly resolve to not hold back. So let it out. Set yourself free.

3. **Rest.** Exhale all of it. The anger. The fear. The hurt. The sadness. Once the anger is released, you will likely feel hurt or sadness arise. Allow these to move as well. Grieve. See if you can feel care and compassion toward yourself for having endured all that has angered and hurt you. Allow yourself as much time as you need to rest and recover.

There are many ways to release anger. It can be helpful to create one's own personally tailored symbolic ritual. Punch a punching bag, tear something, break something, throw something, push something, pull something, bury something, sink something. Find a way. What is important is putting it where it belongs. We have to push back against our perceived abusers and oppressors. Just remember this is an internal process given physical expression in a safe and nonabusive way. Always consider safety measures (punching gloves, pads, safety glasses, etc.) and remember to find time and space where you can be alone and be noisy. ARR is not an exhibition. It's between your own heart and all the forces within you that are bearing down and oppressing you.

Releasing anger is dragon's breath. It is powerful. It is imperative that we be responsible with it. When wielded without care, it can destroy the most precious things in our lives. With care, the fire burns and transmutes what is old and inhibiting and no longer serving us. It breathes new life and power into our experience in the world. It transforms us and sets us free.

Fear

All feelings have value and each feeling has a place. Feeling afraid is not weakness. But denying our fear is weak and ignorant. Fear is the darkness that gives contrast to light. It helps us to know what feels wrong and what feels right. We feel fear when we perceive that something bad is about to happen or when we think something good isn't going to happen. We do this in two ways. One way is healthy and helpful and the other is a neurotic illusion.

Healthy Fear is an obvious warning. It serves us by letting us know we are in danger and helping us avoid unnecessary pain or death. If we become sensitive enough, we can feel a quieter, deeper, more sophisticated fear. This was the fear that generated our night terrors as children and continues to alarm us with disturbing dreams as adults. As children, when the fear-ridden ego began to form, we symbolically witnessed, through our dreams, the loss of our natural sense of safety and connection. As adults, this *Inner Guidance Fear* lets us know when we are stepping away from, or out of alignment with, our true selves. When we heed our inner guidance fear warnings, we stop leaving ourselves and we begin our return to the heart. We stop creating more complex pain and suffering in our lives and instead strive toward ever better-feeling experiences. Listening to inner guidance fear helps us maintain real safety and connection and protect the meaning and joy in our lives.

Neurotic Fear is a bad dream we have yet to wake from. Neurotic fear is the result of incomplete experiences from our past which we continue to live in subjectively. We project this frightening dream onto the current circumstances of our life. When we act on behalf of this fear, we seek to control events and other people. Each action we take on behalf of neurotic fear is a step we take farther away from the true self. The actions motivated by this kind of fear inevitably create more experiences of fear, until we finally let go of control and surrender and finish what is unfinished. Always, when we face this kind of fear, we drop into feelings we were once avoiding and discover an opportunity to continue our journey back to wholeness.

The only way out is through.

Sadness

All roads lead to sadness. Repressive secondary anger guards against layers of vulnerability. Behind the anger is fear and through the fear is pain which is always connected to loss of some sort. At the core of this vulnerability, for all of us, is a deep, abiding sadness that needs release. The emotional system must breathe. We inhale and exhale, take in experience and release experience. When we allow ourselves release of what has finished, there is sadness. While a difficult and painful truth to accept, life is full of sadness. As humans, when we do not understand our anger, we hurt each other. We make mistakes, we change, our friends and family change, relationships change. Everything dies. Plants die, pets die, the people we love die. Everything changes and everything dies and that is tremendously sad.

But without the experience of loss or lack, how could we know the value of any of it? We cannot know the light of day without the darkness of night, and sadness is the night. It is a natural and necessary cycle. Something that we hoped for didn't happen. Something that once was, ceased to be. Or we finally see that something has been missing all along. We realize a lack or loss and there is an awakening. The confrontation with this boundary of loss invites us into relationship with the self. It releases attachment to old limiting self-concepts, so that new, more self-aware ones can be formed. It releases old, inhibiting connections, so that more beneficial ones can be embraced. More simply put, sadness is the breaking open and expanding of the heart.

Acknowledging loss and feeling its accompanying feelings is a way to honor and experience and express deep appreciation for what has passed. It gives us a chance to deepen our understanding of what we now have in our life through intensely focused hindsight. By embracing this hindsight, we are gifted with mature foresight. We can begin to make truly wise and healthy choices, which will benefit ourselves and others. When we stop protecting ourselves from the pain, we can fully acknowledge all that was good of *what was*, with real sincerity. That digested pain inevitably forges within us an authentic and full appreciation of *what is*. And it is only from this point of genuine gratitude that we can truly begin the loving work of honoring what has passed by instilling its freshly distilled meaning into our intentionally created future.

Feeling sadness is sacred. It is sacrifice. It is an offering. It is standing at the edge of the abyss and saying goodbye and letting go forever. When we embrace our sadness and acknowledge its power and dignity, we allow it its rightful place in our human expression as a full-bodied prayer of gratitude. What greater prayer could there be than the tears of the heart cracked wide open, in absolute sincerity and in whatever form, longing for the soul's fulfillment? Our sadness is our soul's testimony of our love. Allowing sadness honors our deepest feelings and our true self. Allowing sadness is loving the self.

Our tears are the melted threads of the veil that blinded us. We try so hard to stave off the awareness or possibility of the end, but only awareness of the end makes what is lasting possible. Let us appreciate the sadness. Our sadness is beautiful. It is the great, resplendent exhale, keeping time and season with the procession of life. It empties us out and makes room for what is more. It bestows wisdom by preparing us to more fully understand, appreciate, and care for all that is to come.

Joy

Joy is freedom. It is the release of limiting constraint on the heart.

As sadness is the exhale, so joy is the inhale. It is the full, inward breath. Recovering what was lost. Redeeming what has been forsaken. Finding what has long been sought. Returning home and questing on. We feel it when we are open to what lies ahead and beyond. Always, joy is fulfillment. It is the soul's incentive to press on.

In the end, joy teaches us that there is a reason and meaning to our suffering. Joy shows us what we have lost sight of or have never seen before. Joy shows us what is true and new and great and glorious. Joy is the knowledge of ever-renewing potential. It is expansion and awakening. It is the great mystery revealing itself at just the right time and in just the right measure. Joy is peering beyond the veil of the world and realizing the infinite. It has no ceiling. It is never as good as it gets. There is always more.

Real joy is grace. Real joy is not something we can seek directly. Grace cannot be obtained by one's own will. By its nature, grace is something to be discovered and appears in its own time. Our experience of joy is the result of an ever-deepening discovery of the meaning of our lives, which can only be distilled by allowing and observing and seeking to understand the natural cycle of emotion. Without anger, fear, and sadness, there can be no joy.

Love

Joy is celebration and love is what we celebrate. Joy is the experience of returning home and love is home. Joy is the mystery being revealed and love is the mystery.

All the different kinds of love—love for our siblings, our parents, our friends, our pets, for our lover, the love we feel for our God, and even the love we feel for our things, all extend from one source in our hearts. At the same time, love is the force creating, sustaining, and changing everything in life. Everything is brought forth and animated by love. There is love in sadness and anger and even fear. Joy is the inhale and sadness is the exhale, and love is the air we breath. We fear losing love or not receiving the love we long for. And the source of the force behind the powerful emotional intensities of anger, rage, and hatred? Love!

Love is the magic contained in every seed and the real source of life radiating from the center of all beings. In humans, love radiates from the heart, and to the degree that we are able to receive it, love brings discerning light and contrast to all our other feelings. We know how dreadful and suffocating our fear is by the degree of expansion and fulfillment we are capable of experiencing in love. Ultimately, our whole experience is brought forth by the macrocosmic source of love, and at the same time, the microcosmic love in our hearts serves as a discerning guide toward our personal wholeness. When our minds are quiet and observing, we can distill this guidance through feeling. Love is always surrounding us and always listening. And when *we* care to listen, love is always willing to speak to us, through feeling.

Love is awareness. We can tell a person we love them until we are blue in the face, but if that person doesn't feel seen and known and understood, he's not going to feel the love. Empathy is the ability to be aware of another person's experience, to hold space for them with our attention and presence. In this way, empathy is love in action. But for most of us, our capacity to be aware of ourselves and each other is limited by our own emotional wounds, by our unfinished feelings. The work of healing those wounds is the path to knowing real love and to being capable of truly loving another. It is a path of healing. A path of empathy, toward the self and the world. It is a path of awareness. Love. Is. Awareness.

Gratitude

Unconditional love is the light radiating from the open heart, and gratitude is the dissolution of darkness slipping into its light. As anger is the force rising to restore balance in the darkness of powerlessness, gratitude is the experience of balance and connection when the light is most high. Anger is the full moon and gratitude is high noon. From the place of gratitude, we see and know that love is flowing through all things. Everything makes sense. Everything has meaning. Hardship has purpose. Challenges we face are more than obstacles, they are signposts showing us the way. And pleasure is more than evolution's incentive, it is grace.

One might normally perceive the feeling of gratitude as the result of joy or the fulfillment of some desired result. But gratitude is really the result of a choice. We can always find something to be grateful for. Our existence is a profoundly absurd miracle. We live on a giant rock traveling thousands of miles an hour around a gigantic perpetually exploding nuclear bomb which, ironically, is giving life to everything that lives within an invisible shield, which is held together by a magnetic field, which is generated by a giant whirling hunk of molten metal at the center of the rock—that's as hot as a nuclear bomb! And all the while, we get to walk and run and jump and see sunsets and hear music and smell flowers and think abstractly and be self-conscious and create and read books and have conversations and have sex! It's freaking crazy! Gratitude is simply waking up to, and recognizing, the truth. Life is amazing.

Looking for gratitude is looking for the truth. The act of looking for gratitude is an inherent duty. It's part of our integrity. If we do not look for this truth, we remain asleep to the wonders of the world. We become vulnerable to all sorts of compromises to our personal integrity. We operate unconsciously, acting from neurotic fears and beliefs and involuntarily recreating them. When we know the truth of gratitude we feel connected and everything is stronger. Our immune system is stronger, our character is stronger, and our confidence, focus, enthusiasm for life, and willpower are all stronger.

Looking for what there is to be grateful for reveals sunlight through the clouded sky. It takes inventory of all our assets and opens the heart to new insight. When we look to be grateful, we are closer to finding the solution to our problem. When we look for lack, we are lost. So when we set out to solve our problem, let us first look for the light that is most high and then look for the solution. Seeking and finding and acting from gratitude inevitably brings more to be grateful for. It returns us to our natural state. It connects us with the flurry of supportive harmony that is always surrounding us, working on our behalf.

When we commit to the practice of relieving our emotional congestion, we naturally arrive at gratitude. When the heart is open, we breathe in gratitude and exhale unconditional love. And we are present in the moment. This is when we are really capable of realizing and experiencing how amazing everything is, right here, right now. It is the state of consciousness we all long for. It is not the result of all our desires being fulfilled or our goals being achieved. It is the result of the choice to look for, remember, and be present with the truth.

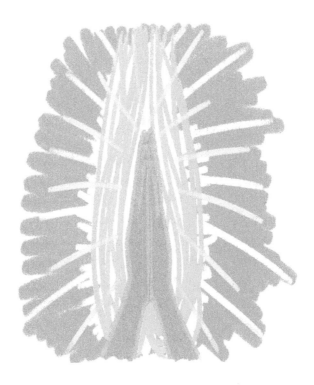

Feeling More Gratitude (SOS)

Look for it! Everyday, in every way, look for it. Make a practice of looking for what there is to be grateful for. Looking for gratitude is an SOS signal to the universe. We are stranded feeling seperate, looking up and out to reconnect. There's no better feeling. It's what we all really want to feel. We can choose to feel it. So practice. Set a clear intention to really allow yourself to feel the truth. Say these affirmations out loud three times: **"I am humble," "I am honest,"** and **"I really want to feel the truth."**

1. **Schedule.** Pick a time of day. Before bed and first thing in the morning are ideal, but you can practice opening the heart all day long. Picking times is a good way to build the habit.

2. **Observe.** Observe whether or not you are emotionally congested. Slow down. Be present with your body. Feel any sadness that needs to be released. It may be masked by anger or hurt at first. Get present with it, breathe and let it move. Express it. Release it. This is acknowledging yourself—caring for yourself. It brings your being back into a state of integrity. Allow yourself to feel grateful for knowing how to do this.

3. **Say thank you.** After you have cleared any congestion, feel your body. Breathe in. Feel grateful for that breath. Say out loud, "Thank you." Move your body. Feel grateful for this amazing vehicle. Breathe in. Say, "Thank you." Look around. Expand your awareness out into the room, breathe in, and feel grateful for the objects in the room, "Thank you." Then close your eyes. Go to all the places where it is easiest to feel gratitude. Breathe in, "Thank you." Feel the people who give to you: friends, family, children, pets, even acquaintances—the person behind the counter serving up your coffee or handing you lunch! Aspire to be thankful for all of the past and hopeful for the future. Breathe in.

Thank you.

*"Let yourself be silently drawn by the strange pull of what you really love.
It will not lead you astray."*

–Jalal ad-Din Rumi

Perceiving Meaning

It is not possible or even desirable to eliminate the challenging feelings and keep only pleasant ones. No one feeling is more valuable than another. They are each elements constituting our chosen alchemy. They're all good. As we journey and create, we discover different combinations and sequences and cycles, which all lead to different feeling-results. We learn and grow and heal and receive the awareness and vision our feelings reveal. This is how we come to know the real value of our feelings: through meaning.

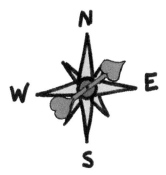

Getting to the meaning means making connections between different points of experience and allowing figures or symbols to emerge that *we feel* make sense. The ability to make these connections is a kind of intelligence that is special to us as human beings. No other animal has this ability. Our ability to discover through contemplation. Our ability to imagine and create. Our ability to perceive without our eyes. Divisive projection is the dark side of this special gift. Realizing connection is its light.

Knowing Your World (7D)

Using symbolism and imagery can be key to making connections that would not otherwise be known. Drawing is a way we can create symbols and imagery from scratch. Drawing has always been an essential part of our evolving intelligence as human beings. It allows us to create, bring form to the formless, and make visible what is unseen, adding new dimension to our experience. Drawing empowers us to quickly share subjective visions and feelings. It can help us to deepen our subjective awareness and discover new insights. Drawing can help us know the self.

Get a large piece of paper and some art supplies: colored pencils, old magazines, scissors, glue, etc. Set a clear intention to really allow yourself to feel the truth. Before you continue reading, say these affirmations out loud three times: **"I am humble," "I am honest,"** and **"I really want to know my world."** Then begin.

1. **Draw a globe.** This is your world. Make sure and leave enough space around the sides so you can draw additional content.

2. **Draw the sun rising in the East.** This is your joy. Along the eastern horizon write, draw, or paste pictures that represent all the joy you are receiving in your life at this time.

3. **Draw the sun setting in the West.** This is your sadness. Along the western horizon write about, draw, or paste pictures that represent all the sadness you are releasing in your life at this time.

4. **Draw the South Pole.** This point represents your fear. Around the south pole write about, draw, or paste pictures that represent all the fear you are experiencing in your life at this time.

5. **Draw dark clouds, the storm, the fire, the full moon**—wherever it shows up. This point represents areas of your life where you experience anger and there is a need to restore balance. Write about, draw, or paste pictures that represent the anger you are experiencing in your life at this time.

6. **Draw the North Pole.** This point represents unconditional love. Around the north pole write about, draw, or paste pictures that represent all the love you are experiencing in your life at this time.

7. **Draw high noon** where the sun shines most bright in your world. This represents your experience of gratitude. Along this path, write about, draw, or paste pictures that represent the gratitude you are experiencing in your life at this time.

This is your world map. It gives a picture of the present condition of your subjective feeling-world. The scenery may be different, but for each of us these areas of feeling-energy and their cycles are always at play. It is not possible or even desirable to eliminate feelings of anger or sadness or fear. It is better to determine how aware we are and how present we can be with these areas and what meaning we can find in them.

Here are some questions to ponder. Read the questions and write down your responses. Take as little time as possible to think about them. Look at your map and write down the first thing that pops in your mind.

What area of my world am I most consumed with?

What feeling is the strongest in my world?

What feeling do I feel the most?

Am I able to be present with all of my core feelings?

Am I fully experiencing the sunrises in my life, the joy?

Am I fully appreciating and experiencing the sunsets, the sadness?

What is my experience of unconditional love in my life?

Do I know true north? What is my highest experience of love?

What is my experience of fear?

What am I a little afraid of? What am I most afraid of?

What are my healthy fears? What are my neurotic fears?

How much does my neurotic fear affect my world?

How much anger do I have? Am I allowing myself to feel my anger?

What is my anger about? Am I stuck in anger? How much time do I spend in anger?

Where does the sun shine brightly in my life?

What are the things I am most grateful for?

Is there gratitude for sadness, anger, and/or fear?

Do I feel stuck or does it feel like I am going somewhere?

How does my map look to me? What do I like best about my world?

What areas need improvement? How do I want my world to look?

Is there a story happening here? Do I like the story?

Who am I? Where am I going? What is the experience I seek from my world?

The meaning of our lives is the story we live and tell. The formation of meaning in one's life forms an umbrella of fulfillment which satisfies the soul, despite any painful feelings we may be cycling through. When we live meaningfully, we discover a deeper level of feeling independent from the outcomes of endeavors or how we are perceived by others. This level of feeling is determined by how we show up, how we consciously choose to meet our life, who we know ourselves to be when we do what we do—whatever we're doing. What we are *being*, regardless of the outcome of the challenges we face, will determine the result of our heart's inevitable feedback. And what we are *being* can only be known through feeling.

Once we uncover and commit to some semblance of meaning in our lives, we cross a threshold. We find a vision and begin the inherent task of manifesting that vision in the world. We transition from the default emotional response of avoiding demise into the default emotional response of pursuing a dream. We have something to fight for, within. And it's a good fight. When we sense and feel the story of our lives, our pain and suffering is not a loss. It has a reason. The burn, the bruise, the bone that breaks, we gladly offer up to what's at stake. We tear in torment and try and fail, but each pain and sorrow stretches us into becoming more than what we could ever know before. And we know it, because we feel it.

When we live meaningfully we are humble. Our ego is restrained by its continual state of rehab as the deeper, heart-driven part of us strives for an ever greater expression of our true self in the world. When we live meaningfully we put away the limited ego-driven story turning in our head and instead adhere to the larger, richer story emanating from our heart. Living meaningfully, we live in *integrity*.

"One does not become enlightened by imagining figures of light,
but by making the darkness conscious."

–Carl Jung

Personal Integrity

 ot the traditional sense of the word integrity. Not adhering to any moral, ethical, religious, or even legal code of conduct, but choosing to act on what feels right and good and true to ourselves as individuals. Sometimes what feels right to the self looks wrong to the world. Personal integrity is adherence to one's own natural, subjective boundaries with the world and constant care for the relationship with one's true self. The practice of personal integrity is a conscious maintenance of the energetic container holding and allowing for expression of the true self. Practicing personal integrity means being in an emotionally committed relationship with the self. Having personal integrity means being whole and unified with the self. It means being contained without breaks or leaks. It means walking in the world as your real self. It means insisting on living free and being something in the world that sets everyone else free. It means having the courage to individuate and celebrate the ways we are all different. It means appreciating the fact that my house is different than yours and embracing the idea that your relationship is different than mine. It means ceasing to measure our individual worth by comparing ourselves to others, but to instead measure the distance between our thoughts and actions, and the silent instruction of our conscience. Not the constructed conscience which was introduced by our upbringing and culture, but an independent conscience, an inherent conscience, which has never been arrived at through deductions of the mind. A *true conscience*, which can only be felt within the heart.

The practice of personal integrity does not mean that we will be celebrated by those around us. In fact almost always when we first step forward into our true self, there is resistance from the people closest to us. Friends, family, spouses, children, parents, employers, and coworkers, who are accustomed to the compromise we have lived in, will feel challenged by the healthy change. This inevitable counteraction is the chrysalis that strengthens our developing self. In this way, the practice of personal integrity differentiates between what feels good and what feels right. But eventually, as we practice acting on what feels right in the heart, good feelings congruent with right actions naturally ensue. The healthy relationships with friends and family adjust to the changes, and in time, they come to see how they benefit from them. The unhealthy relationships fall away.

Growing toward personal integrity is never finished. As healthy, emotion- ally-uncongested humans, our awareness is always expanding. As a result, our personal container is also always expanding. The practice of personal integrity is a commitment to stay honest with the self and continually strive to really show up in one's world. The challenge is to stay living at the brim of our awareness. When we do our best to stay fully present with what we feel at any given moment, we will not likely act, speak, or even think in any way that is incongruent with who we really are. Without the practice of personal integrity, there can be no integrity of any kind. One can only pretend, posture, or placate for so long before the pressure for expression of the real self becomes insuppressible. Eventually, what we are suppress- ing finds a way out. Unwitting verbal slips, surprising angry reactions, passive-aggressive manipulations, and keeping shameful secrets from those we consider closest to us are all examples of suppressed or repressed parts of the self finding unhealthy or unconscious expression. But all of these apparent character flaws, all of what we judge in each other, are actually symptoms of old wounds left untended. Our scandals are simply the pres- surized exhaust of our congested emotional bodies. Rather than judge the exhaust, let us look to the wounds with empathy. If heaven is to descend on the earth it can only come through our collective healing. It can only come through each individual becoming who they truly came to the earth to be.

Improving Personal Integrity (SMART)

Our personal integrity is like a bowl, which holds all that we are. It holds our life-force energy, our feeling of being alive. It holds the allowance of attention and thought-energy we have to work with at any given moment. We cook things up in our bowl. It allows us to focus and think and realize new ideas. It holds who we are and is the vessel through which we give and receive. The condition of this bowl is of paramount importance. We don't want a hole in our bowl! We want our bowl whole! We want to stand tall and know who we are. We want to offer something real when we give. We want to really be able to hold it when we receive.

Attending to our personal integrity is SMART. Everything we struggle with in life ultimately results from compromises to our personal integrity. With a little more honesty and sincere effort, we can become aware of the condition of our bowl. Take some deep breaths and quiet your mind. Set a clear intention to really get to know yourself better. Before you continue reading, say these affirmations out loud three times: **"I am humble," "I am profoundly honest with myself,"** and **"I really want to be true to myself."**

1. **SEER your bowl.** Visualize your bowl. Imagine this is the bowl you use to hold your self. Imagine carrying the substance of your self in this bowl. Imagine it is this bowl that you use to receive everything of value in your life and imagine it is this bowl that you use to give all that you have to give. This bowl contains all the energy you have to focus and concentrate and actively pursue your heart's desires. What is the condition of this bowl? How well is it serving you in your daily living?

2. **Materialize your bowl.** Draw, paint, or sculpt the bowl. Color the bowl. Notice each hole. Notice the little leaks and the larger ones too. Notice cracks. Notice the shape, weight, and material your bowl is made from. Notice how clean or dirty your bowl is. Notice the bowl's contents and how full or empty it is.

3. **Assess your problems.** See if you can label the cracks and leaks. Label the stains. Write down what is contaminating the bowl's contents. Label what is leaking out or what is seeping in. Here is a list of general integrity compromises to help identify the problems:

- **Suppressed Feelings** - A need to release or express feelings that are consciously or unconsciously held back or avoided.

- **Incomplete Communications** - A need to communicate things like apologies, acknowledgments, confessions, or confrontations.

- **Avoided Confrontations** - A need to push back oppressors and establish new boundaries.

- **Requests** - A need to ask for what has too long not been asked for in any relationship.

- **Questions** - A need to clear up any assumptions that have never been addressed in any relationship.

- **Secrets and Lies** - A need to come clean or come out about one's hidden actions and/or true nature.

- **Broken Agreements** - A need to re-establish a commitment so that rebuilding trust can begin.

- **Bad Agreements** - A need to renegotiate old agreements that no longer serve you.

- **Broken or Bad Agreements with Self** - A need to re-establish healthy agreements or identify and re-evaluate old unhealthy agreements with one's self.

- **Physical Health Concerns** - A need seek care for too-long-ignored physical wounds, pain, or discomfort or to address overdue issues pertaining to diet and exercise.

- **Denials** - A need to acknowledge a truth to one's self.

- **Dirty and Messy Spaces** - A need to clean and/or organize any space or material.

- **Debts to Collect** - A need to retrieve money or consciously decide to let it go.

- **Debts Owed** - A need to communicate with lenders and begin paying debt in whatever amount is feasible.

- **Unreturned Borrowings and Lendings** - A need to give things back and/or get things back.

- **Old To Dos** - A need to do it, delegate it, or drop it. Deciding not to do it makes it done. Make a decision.

- **Chemical Addictions** - A need to acknowledge the truth and take steps to get help. Talk about it in a safe place. Find a supportive mentor or sponsor. Find a supportive community.

- **Process Addictions** - A need to talk about it and treat it just like you would a chemical addiction.

4. **Reckon what needs to be done** to improve the condition of your bowl. Imagine how it will feel to have things cleaned up and mended. What actions need to be taken to improve your personal integrity? Make a list of action steps you can take.

5. **Take action!** Put your action steps on your schedule. Sooner is better than later. Little by little, shore up your bowl!

Addiction

Addiction is the result of returning over and over to a behavior that once provided relief but, after too much indiscriminate use, became avoidance. Real relief is like medicine that helps to bring balance so that we can see clearly again and return to the heart. Too much relief is numbing and hindering and puts us at risk for complacency. We lose our path and begin circling in the forest, forgetting the path altogether or believing an aimless circle is the path. Rather than aspiring to create our life to be something that is ever more meaningful and fulfilling, we enter a repeating cycle of pain and avoidance.

Nearly everyone experiences addiction. There are generally two kinds of addictions: process addictions and chemical addictions. Process addictions result from patterns of thinking and feeling that allow for some kind of avoidance of the natural cycle of emotion. There are too many kinds of process addictions to list, but here are a few to illustrate their range (terms in italics are further defined in the *Glossary of Terms*):

Sex	Pornography	Rage
Shopping	Work	Sadness
Overeating	Sleep	*Sarcasm*
Internet	Religion	*Gallows Humor*
Gambling	*Spiritual Bypass*	*Malingering*
Gaming	People Pleasing	*Intellectualization*
Media	Relationships	*Gaslighting*
Exercise	Risk-Taking	*Deflection*

Process addictions are internal processes and behaviors that allow us to avoid being present or connected with the self and others. Process addictions support substance addictions but can exist independent of any substance taken into the body. Many process addictions are unconscious repeating patterns that were established as a result of inevitable childhood trauma. They are individually unique and borne out of the individual's ability to adapt and survive during those hard times. They are not always obvious, and can in fact seem quite normal, but process addictions pale and limit our world and keep us from seeing more of what really is.

Even feelings can become a process addition. The generally angry person, or the generally sad person, may be addicted to those feeling processes. The angry may establish the pattern to avoid feelings of vulnerability and the sad to avoid the possibility of yet another loss. The angry stay angry that they cannot trust, but never get to experience trust because they are so guarded. The sad long for hope and joy but stay focused on loss to avoid another heartbreak. The irony is that trust has to be built with vulnerability and the heart must break so it can expand to hold more and know more of the experience of real joy.

Forming habitual patterns is quite natural and, in many ways, healthy. In order to stop addictive patterns, they must be identified. A very helpful question for exercising this kind of discernment is, "Does this practice take me toward my self or away from my self?" All addictive behaviors take us away from ourselves and eventually lead to anxiety. Another question that can serve to identify addictive behavior is, "How do I feel about myself when I engage in this activity?" However, the questions only work if we are truly honest with ourselves, which is a common challenge to recognizing addictions.

Unchecked process addictions often evolve into chemical addictions. The screen-addicted child, who learned early on to distract himself from his uncomfortable feelings, may eventually find that alcohol offers more effective relief. The codependent sibling, whose emotionally-rescuing big sister moves away to college, finds a new rescuing friend in marijuana. The workaholic who becomes injured on the job is no longer able to lose himself in his work and develops psychosomatic pain in his back which requires prescription opiates, "for the pain." There are endless scenarios in which process addictions can, and often do, lead to chemical addictions. As the pool of unfinished business builds up, there will always become the need for a more powerful method of suppression.

It is also pertinent to note here the relationship between emotional factors and the formation of physical conditions and symptoms. Whatever the drug, the intensity of physiological dependence will be impacted by the state of our neurochemical baseline upon initial use. An extremely repressed individual will have a greater emotional need and thus a greater neurochemical need. This individual will therefore experience greater relief from a chemical substance and be likely to develop a stronger chemical addiction, and develop it faster. In this way, emotional dis-ease is arguably a dominant contributing factor in determining the power of the chemical disease.

Always, freeing ourselves from addiction means tracing our way back through all the feeling-experiences we previously avoided. We have to digest everything we left unfinished. For the long-time addict this task will seem overwhelming as newfound honesty gives way to feelings of shame that are difficult to release. In order to release those difficult feelings we have to talk about them in a safe place and at our own pace, which is daunting. But talking about them and allowing those feelings to wash through the nervous system is good medicine that renews commitment and solders a clean and shiny container for personal integrity.

The path to sobriety is a path of empathy. Having empathy means looking at, or paying attention to, another's experience. It sounds simple, but it is actually a magnificent accomplishment. Before we have the means or capacity to give another our attention in this way, we must first give attention to the self. We must pay attention to our own experience. Instead of avoiding emotional experience, we must choose to stay present, and to feel what we can bear to feel. Instead of overindulging in relief and relieving ourselves from life, we must embrace all the feelings that life serves up and aspire to really live.

Reclaiming Sensitivity

Living free of repression and addiction and allowing emotion its natural ebb and flow inevitably makes us sensitive. Once the tap is opened, we begin to feel more and more. Through our uncongested emotional body, we begin to receive more information from everything we give attention to. We become conscious of the energy flowing through all the objects surrounding us and our lives become richer and more meaningful. The bookshelf is a rainbow of knowledge and experience. Pictures on the walls become portals to their time and place. The naptime blanket is wise with all the dream state journeys of the slumbers it has sheltered for years. An old home echoes with the love it has contained from families past. A hallway floor creaks a cry for the healing of a painful incident unresolved. The morning sun smiles. The sky shelters. The forest whispers. The earth beneath our feet gives and gives and gives.

Sensitivity is not weakness. Sensitivity is awareness. It is required for a deeper perception of self. It is required for a deeper perception of the intricacies of relationship. Without sensitivity, empathy is an impossibility. The retention of one's sensitivity is evidence of one's capacity to bear the pain and suffering that life serves up. It is proof of our choice not to run, repress, avoid, hide, harden, deny, fake, or front. Sensitivity is, in all actuality, testimony to real strength.

"You're too sensitive" is one of the most damaging statements we can make to our children. Usually, we say it because they felt hurt by something we did or said, and since our well-defended ego doesn't want to acknowledge its own hurting child within, we make it about them. We carry on projecting what appears to us as weakness, because we fear feeling the very same pain we see in them. A pain we most likely repressed long ago for fear of the same judgment, we now put on them.

Children need to be allowed their sensitivity. As parents, let us guard our children's sensitivity and seek to learn from it. Our undefended children can feel their true hearts. Their sensitivity can show us the way back to our own. As we aspire to improve our personal integrity, let us strive to increase sensitivity within the self and honor it in each other. Then we will be able to sense the direction we should take in the choices we make to find and fulfill our purpose in life. And we'll be prepared to heed the lessons our little angels have come to share.

Once we have developed a strong and caring connection with the self and achieved some degree of personal integrity, our experience of sensitivity changes. We no longer feel fragile or subject to the emotional winds of the world. There is maturity and stability. We still feel and sense, but we are rooted in the larger, deeper part of ourselves. We are able to observe what we are feeling, as we feel it, without being consumed by it. We stop taking things as personally because we have stopped projecting and we can see projection when it is happening in others. This kind of rootedness is not possible without traversing the natural developmental cycles of sensitivity. When we don't allow our hurt feelings to arise, awareness of our old wounds stay unconscious. We refuse to allow the hurt child within to speak or we refuse to listen. We don't feel the pain and thus remain unaware of our deeper need for healing.

When we retain sensitivity and mature emotionally, we learn to see with the heart. Our sensitivity empowers us to become aware of the underpinnings of everything happening around us, and we begin to see potential outcomes from a long way off. We can then course-correct with intricate navigational knowledge. We come to understand that secrets are an impossibility. All is recorded, no stone is ever really left unturned. Every thought and feeling, every micro choice, every fearful and hopeful breath has contributed to what we are now facing. We awaken to a great truth. Our inner life creates and colors our outer world. So we choose to live consciously and deliberate our inner life with care, and make it true to self—make it beautiful—by making choices we can only make with sensitivity.

*"Your pain is the breaking of the shell that encloses
your understanding.... It is the bitter potion by which
the physician within you heals your sick self."*

–Khalil Gibran

Courage, Fortitude, and the Iphelia Moment

o have courage means to be "of the heart." Having fortitude means being strong and having the capacity to endure pain. To develop empathy and personal integrity, we must become familiar and grow comfortable with a critical moment. It is the moment when fear strikes and we are tempted to avoid feeling and expressing from our true heart. In the beginning, learning to identify this moment is challenging. It starts as a pang of fear, usually when we are thinking about a future event. It can also present as fear when we begin to recall a painful or shameful experience from the past. Either way, we are confronted with an opportunity to traverse fear so we can grow and heal. If we allow this fear to redirect our attention and our behavior, we put off what is inevitable and borrow from our future. We avoid pain but add weight. Our powers of focus, concentration, and memory all suffer. Our capacity for intimacy and emotional range of sensation and expression suffer. We feel happy, but not all of our happiness. We may have glimpses of joy or peace, but they are less enthralling and less frequent.

This is the choice. This is the *Iphelia Moment.* It is the moment we face the choice to stay present and aware and allow the rising core emotional energy to pass through us, or to avoid, deflect, or suppress its natural flow. It is choosing to breathe rather than hold our breath. Choosing to look up rather than look away. Choosing to look inside rather than blame outside. Choosing to be visible rather than hide. Choosing to speak, even if our voice stammers and we turn three shades of red. Choosing honesty, even when we risk losing everything we love. It is choosing to stay and feel and let the soul's bitter potion do its work.

For some of us it can be very difficult to identify this moment. The pattern of avoidance has become so practiced and ingrained that the core feeling, and the fear of it, are not even noticed. Instead there is the illusion of strength, spun by the immediate fearful reaction of anger or rage. But anger is not strength and fear is not weakness. Denying fear hurts the self, and then we cannot help but hurt others we love. We have formed a defense mechanism which will continue until it has caused enough problems in our life that the pain and suffering can no longer be suppressed. Sooner or later we are blessed with a crisis, we hit our bottom, and in that moment we realize *the only way out is through.* Only then will we choose to face our fear and only then can we begin the long awaited work of slowing down, looking inside, and awakening.

The Iphelia Moment is the conscious moment of choice to feel our way toward or away from our true self. When we choose to show up and embrace the moment, we meet the world head on, eyes wide, with erect posture and full breath. We lean into the fear and something magical happens. We connect with life. We live.

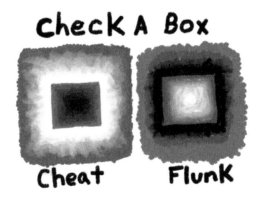

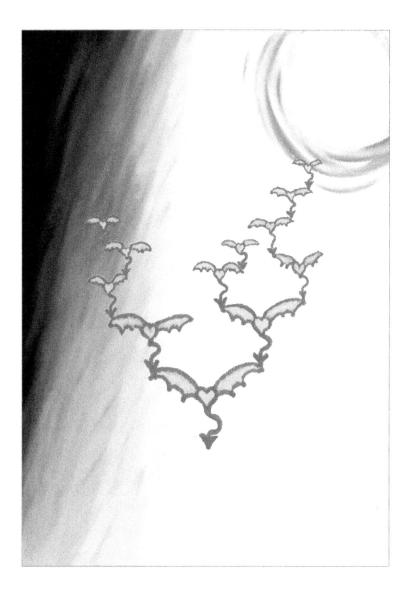

The feeling-experience of our journey is the result of a series of moments and choices. With each choice we navigate toward or away from our true self.

"I am for the house with the narrow gate, which I take to be too little for pomp to enter: some that humble themselves may; but the many will be too chill and tender, and they'll be for the flowery way that leads to the broad gate and the great fire."

–William Shakespeare

Humility and the Trinity Within

umility means being "of the earth." It means knowing one's place in a greater context. It means releasing our defensive delusions and being honest with ourselves. It means being grounded in the truth without projections or assumptions. It means knowing we are not alone. It means having consideration for the other beings of the earth. Humility is not weak. It is not naive. Humility is a virtue. Humility is honest. Humility is not superior. It is not inferior. Humility is powerful. It is receptive and assertive. It is a state of balance. Real humility is only possible when we have released all the defense mechanisms that prevent us from feeling our true heart. Only then can we feel the truth of our predicament. That we are no better off or worse off than any other. That there is much more we don't know about ourselves and our experience than we do know. And that ultimately we are a part of each other and a part of something bigger that we cannot yet conceive, but can only feel.

In relationships, humility accompanies clean empathy. We are allowing there to be a balance between our own experience and the experience of our brother. We cannot know our true place without the ability to feel and accurately perceive the real context of our interactions. This kind of perception is not possible without sensitivity and clean empathy. When we are humble in this way, we are caring for the self within as we meet the world without. We manage internal relationships as we navigate the external relationships in our outer world. We strive to stay in integrity even when we are challenged by the world. This means we aspire toward authenticity and presence. It means we feel our truth when we speak our truth. And it means we are willing to be fully present and fully listen to and feel the truth of our friend. Sometimes this will mean yielding to our friend and to our conscience and sometimes it will mean wielding fierce volition in the face of unjust opposition. But none of this is possible before we are able to truly empathize with the self. In order to practice real humility and real empathy toward the self, it is helpful to become familiar with three basic universal aspects within the self.

The Child

Deep inside of us all is a child who will never grow up. A child who will never become cold or callous. Who is always sensitive and eager and caring. This child is spontaneous, creative, and playful. And always conscious of how wondrous and precious every moment of life is. It's the part of us that breathes fully, sleeps peacefully, and stretches with eager anticipation when we wake. This part is innocent and forever lives with an open heart, however painful it may be. It has no tendency to avoid or escape. It always seeks to connect. It is the part of us that recognizes we are all children subject to a universe forever older and more knowing than we can ever be. It is the humble part, the beautiful part. This child lives in our heart, and reconnecting with it helps us to know who we really are.

Like an onion, our personality develops in layers. And like an onion we have to peel through the layers to get to the core. At our core the child part of us lives undefended. Surrounding the pure and innocent core are layers of fear-driven defense mechanisms. The defenses formed to protect the core layer during the early years, but later, when they are no longer necessary, they blind and inhibit us. These layers continue to glom on and crystallize further until we finally become tired of the pain and suffering they cause. Life loses its luster. Attempts to connect keep failing. The same painful thing happens over and over again in our relationships. Eventually we bump our heads enough times and there is an awakening. Our attention turns around and looks inward. We introspect. We begin to pay attention to ourselves, to our own inner process. A personal authority begins to develop and our growth, rather than something carried forward by the natural procession of life, becomes ever more conscious and self-directed. We become self-determined. We begin to understand the meaning of responsibility. We realize we have the ability to respond. We have choice. That no matter what happens to us in the outside world, or what old pain emerges from within, we can decide how we meet that challenge. We can decide how we suffer. Kicking and screaming and flailing about, or chin up and chest out. We always have the opportunity to reach for the core. We always have choice.

The Mature Adult

Once the adult self begins to develop, it becomes our inherent task to heal the layers concealing the light radiating from our core. Neglecting this task compromises our personal integrity, the consequence for which is an ever more burdensome background shame that drives addiction and avoidance in all its forms.

The adult self is the thickest, outermost layer. It is developing right now. Every introspective thought, every conscious intention, every connection made in contemplation, and every practiced expression all influence its formation. A healthy construct that is formed little by little one day reaches a critical mass, and a major shift in the personality occurs. We stop blaming. We shift from viewing life as something that is happening to us, to something we are happening to. We discover the connection between our relationship with the self and our relationships with all the world. We realize we can learn to care for the self in all the ways we missed out on and we discover power. Instead of focusing on what is out of our control, we shift our focus to what we can influence and establish a path to greater empowerment. We begin to see more than we ever did before. Creativity unveils choices that had never been considered. Obstacles that once seemed impossible become vulnerable to simple solutions. And if nothing can be done to avoid the undesired outcome, we savor the most precious opportunity of all by deciding how and what we will be as we meet our suffering.

Once we turn inward, stop blaming, and shift to empowerment, the mature adult is firmly established. The mature self observes without reacting unconsciously. It operates in the present and in the relevant context. In other words, it does not project. It doesn't unconsciously play out any old unresolved experiences, or if it starts, it catches itself. The old feelings may be present. We might be triggered by something and really feel it. But the mature adult knows it's triggered and knows how to tend to those feelings in a way that brings healing, and refrains from recreating the same old drama.

The adult self is the layer of consciousness we develop that is non-reactive and makes healthy choices to care for our feeling heart. The adult self manages our engagements with the outer world and with old inner defense mechanisms in a healthy way. Like any good parent, the mature adult meets the feelings of fear or sadness with feelings of care and support toward the hurt child layers. Feelings of sadness and grief are honored and allowed full expression. Feelings of hurt are not avoided, but felt fully and soothed.

Messages from healthy fear are heeded. Feelings of neurotic fear are fully acknowledged and there begins encouragement toward possible ways of facing the fear. As the mature adult develops, this process evolves and becomes an automatic response, which, in time, strengthens our personal integrity and our capacity for real connection with others. As we return to a pattern of allowing the natural cycle of emotion, establish our adult self, and connect with our child self, there becomes an ever-increasing recollection and utilization of a long-lost resource that has always been available.

The Higher Self

The mature adult self appears to be formed by a combination of factors. Genetic predisposition and the positive experiences we have had with healthy adults give us a starting point. We strive to emulate the best of what we've known. But nature and nurture are really only the most obvious scenery. Always in the background is an ever-present feeling, calling from the core, guiding us toward maturity. The development of the mature adult is the result of releasing congested feeling-energy that is in the way of following that inner call. It is the consistent choice to follow the feeling of what is true to our individual nature. In the beginning this is a relatively clumsy and unconscious process. But practiced over time, we become more aware of the subtleties that make up our subjective reality. Through persistent alignment with this feeling-guidance from within, we eventually develop a unique and personalized version of a mature adult. In our own individual way, we grow wise. We see more and instead of always avoiding and consuming, we aspire to be more. Through finishing what is unfinished, we begin to feel more and start to make more conscious choices, which eventually establishes a direct and communicable relationship with the higher self.

This is the original irony. It is the origin of all the irony we face in life. Intimate knowledge of the true source of our real freedom and power lies at the same core we have covered up and are defending. Our projected neurotic fear guides our crazy choices, recreating the circumstances that reinforce the fear we began with. We blindly look outward for an answer that can only be found within. In order to stop this perpetual cycle and awaken from the dream of separation we have to face fear and practice faith. We have to feel.

Some of us are fortunate enough to be born to parents who model feeling-awareness and this can give us a head start, but in order to develop an authentic, healthy, mature adult, there must always be the discovery of one's own inner knowing. Our inner knowing speaks to us through feeling. The core is always transmitting feeling-messages that guide us toward inner stability and personal integrity. When we allow ourselves to become quiet inside and listen within, we can receive these inspiring and uplifting whispers of truth. Then the projection of separation dissipates. And as we allow ourselves to be present with and feel the forces of nature that surround us, we can recognize symbolic metaphors, revealing wisdom and meaning for relevant circumstances in our lives. In the beginning we may only see a flicker of this inspired awareness here and there. The goal is to stay conscious and strive for a steady burn.

As above, so below. As within, so without. This sequence of connection from higher self through the adult self to the child self is the symbolic design of each individual orb of consciousness. It is also the natural and literal model for supporting children in developing healthy personalities capable of real connection and empathy. There are outlying factors but, by and large, we unconsciously internalize the setting we grow up in. We learn to relate to ourselves the way our parents related to us as children. If our parents care for our feelings and connect with us we learn to feel and be connected. If our parents are disconnected and addicted, we learn to avoid feeling and seek our own addictions. The condition of our parents' devotion to a higher principle can even determine our starting feelings about spirituality and our own higher self. Even though we may fight hard to resist the beliefs and conditions that are put on us, we cannot help but internalize some befuddled version of that process of resisting. If we grow up in fear-driven obedience to religious doctrine, we might be drawn to our own non-direct connection, or reject religion, spirituality, and the relationship with our higher self altogether. Growing up in an environment where there are genuinely practiced spiritual principles, we may resonate with the integrity surrounding us and find encouragement to later embrace the same or find some spiritual practice of our own choosing, which promotes introspection and leads us to inner connection sooner.

Ultimately, establishing an authentic connection with our higher self will require that we accomplish some degree of excavation through the layers of separation covering our child self. Then, when we are sensitive enough and quiet enough to listen to the deeper heart, within the heart of our inner child, we can connect. We may also connect when we are quiet enough to feel the deeper heart of other living beings. And some of us may look out and up, as high as we can, and project the deeper heart of our child into the ether, and that projection might actually attune us to the larger heart of the macrocosm. In any case, and in all forms, connecting with the higher self requires personal empathy and in turn, clean empathy, *to feel* and know what is greater.

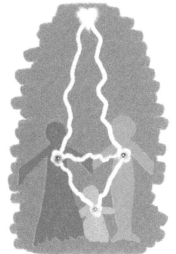

"Between stimulus and response there is a space.
In that space is our power to choose our response.
In our response lies our growth and our freedom."

−Victor Frankl

Iphelia Moments Within

s we grow and become ever more conscious, we see that Iphelia Moments are happening all the time. An Iphelia Moment waits when we face a stressful turn of events that we'd really rather not deal with. When we are put on the spot to make a life-altering decision, an Iphelia Moment greets us. Iphelia Moments arise when our children ask us profoundly simple questions about life. When we decide whether or not to admit a mistake, make amends, or even tell the truth about something we lied about, Iphelia Moments happen. And all the while, these moments are occurring in our own subjective thoughts and feelings. Recognizing and meeting them requires unique strengths and skills that need to be developed.

To notice Iphelia Moments, we have to be alert and present and feeling. When we miss the moment, we act out of habit or with an old defense mechanism. An old, unhealed part of ourselves takes the driver's seat and we act unconsciously. Noticing these moments requires that we slow down and introspect, while staying present with what we are feeling. Then we can notice choices about how we are going to orient our perception toward something: choices about which voice in our head we will listen to, about what feelings we will project onto ourselves and onto the circumstances of our world.

Often these choices can be reduced to the play between our developing adult self and our wounded child self. The question becomes, "Are we focusing on our adult self or allowing old hurt child parts to run the show?" Being ready when these moments of conflict arrive requires practice and preparation.

As an adult, resolving conflict within the self is always the responsibility of the self. It is never another person's job to make everything okay for anyone else. Maintaining integrity of the self is the responsibility of our adult self, and so is getting to healing. When conflicts arise within the self it usually involves a hurt child aspect; part of us that was hurt as a child and has not yet healed or fully developed reacts. This is when our projections can really kick in, and we begin thinking the way to feel better is to get someone on the outside to do something different.

Despite what our projections would have us believe, the only solution that can ever have a lasting effect is keeping in touch with our adult self when we get triggered. Then we can provide personal care for our hurt child. We learn to soothe and advocate for the hurt child in a mature and empowering way. Soothing and advocating for our hurt child is something most of us struggle with because we did not receive that as children. By learning to relate to ourselves the way our parents related to us, we inherited a pattern of shame and blame from the chain of insensitive chaos that was our family's history. But moment by moment, the hurtful legacy can come to an end. If we can stay conscious of our inner process, we can notice the opportunities to soothe and care and resolve the conflicts within. We can practice truly loving ourselves and healing ourselves in these most critical moments. We can cease to project and blame and stop perpetuating the pain we endured as children.

Strengthen Up Mature Adult (SUMA)

Here's a practice for strengthening the connection with the wise and mature adult within. Take some deep breaths and quiet your mind. Set a clear intention to really get to know yourself better. Before you continue reading, say these affirmations out loud three times: "I am profoundly honest with myself," "I really want to know my whole self," "I really want to know the wise and mature parts of myself."

1. **See the strength.** Take inventory of all the wise-healthy-mature adults you know in your life or from film, history, or literature. These are your examples. Here it can be good to include times when you have really felt yourself being a strong adult but it also helpful to stretch and reach for more with external examples. This is a positive use of projection. What you see in your examples are actual resources you already possess within. See them in your mind. Remember times when you thought highly of your examples. What were they doing or saying? How were they being? Write down the qualities and/or virtues they embody. Be specific. See if you can really distill what inspires you about them.

2. **Utilize the strength.** Pick your top five qualities. Take a minute with the first one. Close your eyes. Imagine what it is like to embody that quality. Position your body the way you see your resources positioned in your mind. Breathe the way the resource breathes. Say something, speaking the way the resource speaks. Feel that confident, disciplined, strong, or wise—whatever is on your list—be that quality. Count them out. Using your dominant hand, extend a finger for this quality. When you have felt the essence of that quality, even if for only a moment, move on to the next one. Continue until each of the five fingers on your hand are extended.

3. **Make a fist.** Bring them all together now. Feel them all together, all one. Like the ingredients of the perfect soup all together, hot on the stove. Get a whiff. Feel what it feels like to be that ideal, wise, mature adult. Breathe with it. With each breath, tune more and more into the whole body experience of your mature adult self.

4. **Anchor your feelings.** Allow a word or a phrase to come to you which represents this experience of the wise adult. Allow a symbol to come to you. Allow a color to come to you. Pack it all together. The fist, the feelings, the phrase, the symbol, and the color. This will be the talisman which helps you connect to your own wise, healthy, mature adult.

The list helps us to identify the projected parts of our self that we want to get in touch with. These are parts we have suppressed or are just now beginning to develop. The SUMA practice is helpful for building a psychological anchor that can instantly put us back in touch with the adult part of ourselves when the hurt child part gets triggered. This way, anytime we want to reconnect with the wise and mature adult, we can just make a fist and come right back to our senses!

Love On Connected Kid (LOCK)

Once the adult self is firmly established, we can begin to apply the medicine. Here is a very simple practice for soothing and healing the old wounded parts of the self. In the beginning, this practice can be like learning to eat with chopsticks. You may feel awkward and get distracted by old negative defenses, but with persistent practice, this can become a new habit and eventually form a permanently rooted way of relating to the self.

Set the intention. Affirm out loud or to yourself three times, **"I am an adult," "I am completely responsible for what I am feeling," "I care for my child self," "I listen to myself and allow myself to feel."**

1. **See your child self** in your mind and stay present with the core feeling. Finding a picture of yourself as a child can help with this, preferably a picture when you are age seven or younger. You need to see yourself at an age before too many defense mechanisms formed so you can really see the innocence and sensitivity. Then consider these questions: What would you say to the child? How would you say it? What are you feeling when you speak to the child?

2. **Allow feelings** to move. Feel the sadness. Allow it to pass over you. Cry. Moan. Say out loud what the feelings are saying. These are the cries of the hurt child. Say out loud what you need to say to your child self. Give it expression. All of it.

3. **Do something to nurture yourself.** Soothe yourself. Express positive feelings toward your child self. Put your hands on your heart and feel yourself sending love. Take a bath, take a walk, take a nap, take a vacation, meditate, listen to inspiring music, draw, hug a teddy bear, play, create. Be with yourself in whatever way helps you remember who you are and feel really great about who you are. Then, as you move about your day, practice continuing to hold feelings of care

and support toward yourself. Really allow yourself to feel great love for your child self within. Strive to make those feelings a part of your everyday way.

This is the quintessential point of healing for us all. Conscious improvement of the relationship between the child self and the adult self eventually becomes imperative. The aim is not to forever become completely autonomous and never need the care of another. But it's good to know we could if we wanted to. Then we can begin to set healthy boundaries and shape our relationships into truly supportive connections. Knowing how to care for the self allows us to know what real care is. Without knowing what real care feels like, we can't recognize who is healthy and who is not. It's a law of physics—metaphysics. We will be drawn to, and attach ourselves to, what is most reflective of our own inner process. That's what will seem most familiar, comfortable, and deserving to us. So before we can expect any relationship to improve in our outer life, we have to first look to the condition of our inner relationship with our most vulnerable self.

*"People will forget what you said, people will forget what you did,
but people will never forget how you made them feel."*

–Maya Angelou

Iphelia Moments in Relationship

mpathy is the medicine that will heal the world. All of our conflicts arise out of a lack of empathy—when there is a lack of awareness and understanding of each other's experience. Once we have achieved some degree of personal integrity, our capacity for clean empathy is established. Then we can look at our friends, family members, and even our perceived adversaries and see them in a new light.

Love On Other Kid (LOOK)

LOOKing is empathy in action. In order to effectively LOOK we have to be able to sustain an open heart, which means we have to be SUMA LOCKed. If fear floods through the heart and mind, the attention will dart around in an anxious flurry and leave no room for empathy. Instead, we will project our own hurt and fears onto the situation and our actions will perpetuate the cycle we are attempting to change. So check in to see if a SUMA LOCK is needed before having a LOOK.

Set the intention. Affirm to yourself, **"I am an adult," "There is a child within me," "There is a child within my friend," "I care for my child self and I care for the child of my friend."**

1. **See the child and the adult** of your friend in your mind. Strive to see the innocence and sensitivity in the child aspect. Strive to see the maturity and strength in the adult aspect. Imagine your friend's capacity to care for and support her own child self.

2. **Observe the connection** between the child self and the adult self. What do you perceive the child is feeling? Is there an adult present? How strong is the adult self? And most notably, what is the condition of the relationship between the adult self and the child self?

3. **Feel the child and the adult.** Empathize. Find the part of your self that resonates with what you perceive before you. Feel it. Consider what you want to say to the child. Most importantly, consider how you would say it. What are you feeling when you speak to the child?

4. **Tend to the hurt child,** and perhaps talk to the adult. Try to be aware of which part is present in your friend at any given moment when speaking to her. Express gentle and positive feelings toward the child self. Express strengthening and affirming feelings toward the adult self. Strive to speak to your friend in a way that supports and encourages the connection between her adult self and child self.

Sometimes, you'll realize that a friend is truly impaired by the lack of an adult ego state. In such cases, tending to the hurt child may mean setting immediate and clear boundaries. In rare instances when there is absolutely no adult present in your friend, you may need to set a quick and firm boundary without explanation. Interacting with these individuals can feel very much like interacting with a child having a tantrum, or even an infant who is unable to comprehend the situation or control his own impulses.

The Blessing of Boundaries

In many traditions throughout history, the open-palmed hand has been the symbol of protection, healing, and blessing. It also means stop. Here, the symbol is used to portray the focus of attention and intention when navigating Iphelia Moments in relationships.

Setting healthy boundaries is blessing and protecting the highest good of all concerned. When our adult self is present, we can aspire to set boundaries in a spirit of protection, healing, and blessing. Healthy boundaries support our self and our friend. When the adult ego state of our friend is underdeveloped, setting healthy boundaries can help him make critical inner connections that have not yet been formed. This is extremely helpful to those of us who have yet to establish an adult self. It helps us find our outer limit and begin our own inward turn—begin introspection. Children need adults to set boundaries with and for them. This is how they learn self-restraint and self-discipline, how they learn to set boundaries with themselves. Adults who are still behaving like children need boundary experiences. If boundaries are never set, they do not reach the critical point of introspection and the adult doesn't develop. When we set healthy boundaries, we give a burdensome interaction meaning and provide ourselves with an opportunity to

further strengthen our own mature adult self. When we set healthy boundaries, we advocate for our child within and support the child within our
friend. There is growth and forward motion. And we can feel it.

All relationships require boundaries and limits. The most intimate and
trusting relationships maintain clear and healthy boundaries. Establishing
boundaries establishes the unique characteristics of the container that will
support the integrity of each person and the integrity of the relationship.
Without boundaries, there can be no containment or integrity.

Real boundary-setting begins energetically—in our consciousness. It is
something we first do with our attention. Subtle boundaries are established
and maintained by our thoughts and feelings and unconscious behaviors.
They are established by what we give attention to or withhold it from. What
we choose to think and feel about. What we entertain or ignore. What our
being engages in or is silent to. Usually, before any situation becomes large
enough to require outer boundary-setting, we have either let the experience
become too big by not noticing ways we have relaxed our subtle boundaries,
or we have grown in some way and now desire healthier boundaries than
were previously in place. When considering setting boundaries, we need
to look inward and identify subjective contributing factors to the difficulty
we are facing. If we do not recognize what needs to change on the inside,
we will inevitably become frustrated with what, despite self-perceived
repeated efforts, is not changing on the outside.

Setting a new boundary will always begin with identifying a point of choice
in which we either protect and uphold or compromise our sense of freedom
and empowerment. It means finding where we can make a choice that keeps
our child self safe and keeps our personal integrity intact. This point always
exists, but often we are not able to see it right away because of old neurotic
fears or attachments that are still blinding us.

Defining the Lines (3D)

Here's a practice for figuring out what your boundaries are. Take some deep breaths and quiet your mind. Set a clear intention to find a choice you could make that would improve your experience of the situation or relationship in question. Say these affirmations out loud three times: "I am profoundly honest with myself," "I am the creator of my experience," "I really want to see," "I really want to know the choice that can set me free."

1. **Dream.** Allow yourself to have a fantasy of how your life would be if you could have it be the way you want it to be. Be simple with the changes you make. Visualize a dream where you feel really-really-really good about yourself, but be minimal in the changes you make in the circumstances of your present life. The operative requirements here are personal safety and personal integrity. So only imagine the changes necessary to invoke the better feeling. Begin to notice what's different. What habits are different? What perceptions are different? What unspoken agreements are different? What spoken agreements are different? What behaviors are different?

2. **Determine the aspect** or aspects of your experience you desire to change so that you can experience the better feeling place. Become aware of what specifically needs to change. Then ask yourself this question, "What can I personally do differently to ensure my experience changes?" There is always an answer to this question. The answer has nothing to do with any other person's behavior. Ask this question for every aspect of your experience that is causing emotional discord. Write down all the answers. It is very likely that some answers will challenge you to face some long-standing, unacknowledged fears.

3. **Decide what you are going to do and do it.** Look at your list. Read through it and pay attention to how you feel as you consider each

possibility. Which choice gives you the most energy or excitement when you consider it? Decide what you are willing to do. You might decide to ask for what you want. You might decide to do what you know you need to do and let things play out. Make the choice and follow through. Take one more step toward being true!

Finding this point of choice inevitably awakens us to an Iphelia Moment. Setting a boundary, whether with the self or another, is usually a kind of confrontation. We are defining our outer edges. We are sculpting space for the self. Each conscious choice is a chiseled point on a line, in a pattern with many lines, forming the unique multidimensional structure of our personal container.

Establishing boundaries is changing the flow of an energy pattern. In relationships, this means we have to be consistent with doing what we say we are going to do. In order to do this, we have to be consistent in how we think and feel. We have to practice staying conscious and making choices congruent with our true self. Only then, like a fully mature adult or parent, do we have the strength and fortitude to follow through with consistency and facilitate the change.

Our boundaries in relationships are dynamic. As we grow and change and the people in our lives grow and change, the boundaries may change. Increased self-awareness and personal integrity deepen our understanding of what is healthy. And in time, we develop the courage and fortitude to set clearer and healthier boundaries. We grow and see more, see and grow more. Eventually we can arrive at a place of real freedom and empowerment. In the meantime, making the choices we have the strength to make is enough.

Setting Boundaries with the Self

When we feel trespassed against or compromised in some way, old defense mechanisms will very likely kick in. We might have a tantrum and start throwing our weight around. This might give some immediate relief, but is ultimately unproductive because it hurts our relationships and we keep suffering. We might also be tempted to stay quiet in an effort to keep the peace and avoid confrontation. This leads to more emotional congestion within the self and blocks real intimacy and cooperation in relationships. These extreme reactions, and all the possibilities between, represent various forms of the old lizard brain, fight or flight, way of surviving. But most of the situations we are reacting to would be better handled with the larger, newer parts of the brain and with the heart. If we are to keep from devolving back to survival mode, we have to stay present, feel our feelings, and practice resolving our inner conflicts. Then we have a real chance at effectively facing and resolving the conflicts in our lives.

Problems in our relationships arise when actions are taken based on negative assumptions about the other's behavior: "He did that because he doesn't care about me," "She did that because she wants to control me." These assumptions happen between all kinds of human organisms—businesses, religious groups, political groups, countries, races, and individuals. The assumption, whether true or not, generates fear and a perceived lack of safety. Left unchecked, these feelings of fear often lead to behaviors that eventually hurt ourselves and others. If we are to interrupt this pattern, bringing the assumption into the light is imperative.

When outer conflicts arise, it can be wise to first seek awareness of any conflicts within the self, before acting. After we have achieved a sufficient degree of consciousness about our inner conflicts, we can proceed to address outer conflict in a meaningful way.

Conflict Projection Resolution (CPR)

In order to resolve inner conflict, we have to FIND the projection. Conflict is always an opportunity to more fully show up in our lives. It gives us a chance to face fear that would otherwise continue unconsciously holding us back. Sometimes, facing this fear will be taking new, courageous action in the world and sometimes it simply means being courageous within ourselves and feeling our unfinished feelings. Either way, facing this fear always means being profoundly honest with ourselves. Resolving the conflict might be entirely subjective, looking within at what we would rather not see about ourselves, acknowledging old wounds, and deciding what needs to be done to heal them. Or the opportunity for resolution can take a more dramatic form when we are given a chance to acknowledge our much-feared inner resources and face the potential consequences of embracing them. We realize an Iphelia Moment, and we are given a choice to use our voice and speak our truth—to set healthy boundaries and improve our life circumstances. In any case, to heal and grow, we have to find the projection and the assumptions we are making about people and the world.

Set the intention. Affirm to yourself, **"I am an adult,"** **"I am totally responsible for what I am feeling,"** **"I am totally responsible for my emotional needs."**

1. **Feel the core feeling** (what is behind the anger). Sit with the anger until you can feel the deeper feeling that happened before the anger. Ask yourself, "Am I feeling hurt, sadness, or fear under my anger?" Notice where you feel the feeling in your body. Why does it hurt? Staying present with the feeling allows it to deliver its message. Be it something recent or something we've plugged into from the past, if the feeling is happening, there is something that needs to be done.

2. **Identify the Experience and the Assumption.** Ask yourself, "At what moment did I become triggered? What is the perceived trespass that caused this intense feeling to rise? What happened in the recent situation? What does it mean about me? What does it mean about the other person? What am I assuming about the other person? What do I assume they think or feel about me or the world?"

3. **Notice the Projection.** "What does this experience remind me of? What other experiences in the past have happened that felt just like this?" And the most important question of all: "How does this conflict reflect the conflict I have within myself?" This information is helpful for identifying the source of projections, soothing the hurt child within, and deciding whether or not to clear the assumption with the party in question.

4. **Decide.** At this point, you must decide what kind of resolution the situation calls for. Does it feel complete to have identified the projection within the self? Do you feel balance returning within the self? "What practice can I implement to improve my relationship with the wounded part of myself?" By identifying the projection and owning it, you have already taken a critical step toward containment, toward personal integrity. "Are there still actions that need to be taken to further shore up or strengthen my personal integrity?"

At this point, your CPR may be complete. If you have identified the projection and, after having a LOOK, recognize that it was completely your bag, then there is no need to do anything in the relationship. Doing anything more, outwardly, has become unnecessary, because you have released the projection. Resolution is completed within the self. As you soothe your own hurt child, strive to feel gratitude for the interaction that has brought the new awareness and potential healing. You may choose to share your experience with your friend, but it is not necessary. The energy has moved. You are complete.

Outer Resolution

Soothing our hurt child within is an inherent part of resolving projections within the self. What to do next requires some discernment. Here is the operative question: *Is there an adult self in my friend?* If there is an adult present, we can decide to really show up and communicate to resolve the projections that are harming healthy connection and intimacy in the relationship. Again, if we are not perceiving an adult, focusing solely on establishing healthy boundaries is probably best.

Generally, seeking outer resolution is not helpful to do with anyone who doesn't have some semblance of a developing mature adult. But when there is an adult present in relationships, it is a courageous and necessary action to meet the conflict by communicating about what we are experiencing. We have to move what is in the way out of the way so we can see each other again. This means clearing assumptions and projections. It means, in a very mature and caring way, calling ourselves on our shit and calling our friends on theirs. It means recognizing when we are not seeing our friends clearly and giving them a chance to see us.

Assumptions, whether they are true or not, rise out of fear and a perceived lack of safety. They rise from the old hurt child layers of consciousness.

When we don't clarify our assumptions, they cause an energetic congestion that colors our perception. Even if we try and hide the way we feel, our assumptions and projections guide our behavior in unconscious ways. The energies find their own way to move, making little micro choices here and there, recreating experiences analogous to the past from which they originated. Eventually, this old dream becomes so cumbersome that we, in some way, begin to hurt, or we hurt someone we really care about.

The only way to stop this pattern from manifesting is to interrupt its cycle. Instead of repressing, we have to feel. If we are to interrupt the pattern instead of acting on the assumptions and projections, we have to bring them to light for all the parties involved. So whether it is true or not, we must ask, "Do you care about me?" "Are you trying to control me?" And when we ask, we must ask from the heart. We must feel the feeling from where the question originates. No two organisms can achieve a successful understanding of one another through a mere linear exchange of information. Simply reporting that we are feeling hurt or sad or afraid is not enough. The energy must move. The feeling must be felt as the words are dealt. This is what it means to emote, to move. Only when there is real movement does real communication take place. Otherwise, nothing has changed. When we face our Iphelia Moment, stay present with the original core feeling, and share our truth, we release light into the world. We give our friend an opportunity to see and feel what we are experiencing and an opportunity to see and feel what she may have done. We give her the opportunity to meet her own Iphelia Moment.

The following is meant to be a guide and a reminder, not a formula for success. It is a path of intent. The steps are points of focus. It is not possible to formulate a sure template for resolving conflict. Conflict exists for a reason. Resolving conflict is an evolutionary process. Real resolution is creative and original. Necessity stretches us into some place new, especially within the self and between ourselves and others. Polarities within the self birth awareness of something new, something more—another way of thinking, feeling, seeing, and being. At the same time that we are becoming more, new collaborations happen between us and the world. We find new ways of relating and cooperating and learning and teaching. New ways of seeing and supporting each other. As we accept all of ourselves, we accept all of each other. As we accept each other, we discover new parts of ourselves we've never known before. When we identify our inner conflicts, become aware of the polarities, and stay present with the struggle, we can discover and incorporate what is new. We can evolve. This universal process is the center of our individual and collective healing and growth.

The CPR CALL

Many practices have been developed to manage and resolve conflicts between individuals and groups and organizations. But for us to utilize any of these methods and be effective, we have to show up in integrity. We have to show up authentically. Otherwise, we are just pretending or posturing, which adds more layers to the problem of real communication. Showing up in integrity means acknowledging that we are fully responsible for the condition of our side of the street and being authentic in our expression. This means we care for our kid. It means our adult self advocates for our hurt child self. It means we can feel our pain and show it, without throwing our kid in another's lap. We keep our adult present and stay present with what we are feeling when we speak our truth. This kind of vulnerability can be one of the most challenging experiences we ever face. We are best prepared to face it in a genuinely safe place. Therefore, it is highly recommended that one perform a SUMA LOCK LOOK before attempting a CPR CALL.

Set the intention. Affirm to yourself, "I am humble," "I am genuine," "I care for myself and others in a good way," "I honor myself and others when I speak my truth."

1. **Clear the assumption.** Hold the core feeling, share your experience of the trigger, and clarify the assumption. This is very important. You must show up feeling from your core and not from a hiding place or suppressing with secondary anger. A CPR CALL requires a full breath, an authentic breath. This is not regressing back to a child state. The adult self is present, advocating for the hurt child within the self and within your friend. It is not an opportunity to attack or vie for control. It is a sincere inquiry. Ask your friend if it's true, "Am I not important?" "Do you want to control me?" "Are you lying to me?" "Do you want to hurt me?" Then listen. Listen on the level of feeling. Unless you have more assumptions to clear, there is no need to respond to the answers. Just listen and thank the person for hearing you. You have moved the energy. Release it. You have advocated for yourself. You have spoken on behalf of the hurt child deep inside and you have let your brother or sister know what your experience has been. Their experience of your sharing is theirs. Any counter-projections are not your responsibility to fix or fight. Even if you perceive resistance or denial from the person you are sharing with, you don't need to argue. Let it simmer, give your brother or sister time to process what you have shared. If nothing changes, you can clear again.

2. **Ask for what you want.** Sometimes this can happen immediately. Sometimes it takes time to get to this step. Share what you would like to experience. Whatever the trigger was, ask for what would be better next time. "Can you please stop making fun of my drawings?" "Can we spend more time together on Saturdays?" "Can you please ask me before you eat one of my Twinkies?" For more intimate relationships, this may also be a time when we want to share some of the content of our inner experience. This is not to burden the person or make them responsible for your experience but to help those who really care for us be aware of us, allowing them to more fully understand what our experience was and have a chance to experience more empathy.

3. **Let them know what you are going do and do it.** At this point, pay attention to what you feel you need, from yourself, to take care of yourself. Remember, it's not about getting this other person to change. What you have just done is helping you get to know the other person and get to know yourself. So you might strike a new agreement, or you may just have to set your boundaries. Tell them, "I'm not showing you my drawings for a while," "I'll ask you a week in advance when I want to spend time with you," "I'll find someone else to spend time with," "I'm locking up my Twinkies." Say what you're going to do, then do it. Caution: letting them know what you are going to do is never a threat. It is truly informing your friend of what you intend to do in response to what you now know. That is all.

4. **Let go.** There is no power struggle here. Surrender any need to control anyone else's behavior. Only be concerned with your own actions. Once you have committed to your decided actions, the only thing left is to follow through and that is between you and you. At this point your actions are about taking care of yourself and supporting others in knowing your boundaries. Do what you said you would do. Once you are complete on your side of the street, it is done.

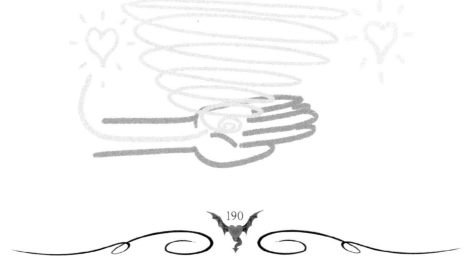

A true CPR CALL is intimacy. It is authenticity. It is not a power struggle. The only point of control is in managing one's own fear. Releasing projection is releasing the need for control. It is surrendering to the truth. It is allowing emotional energy to move in a conscious way, in a good way, in a responsible way.

The CPR CALL is a skill that takes practice to develop. Don't worry if you don't do it perfectly. In the beginning, it can be messy, because we may struggle with SUMA and LOCK and may not be comfortable staying present with our feelings and sharing them. And sometimes things are just going to be messy because the healing is very deep or because we haven't been breathing or feeling or communicating for a while. There's a lot to cough up!

When we stay with our core feelings and speak authentically, we let others see what is happening inside of us. This is, in all actuality, a beautiful thing, but our egos might want to call it messy. If it feels messy afterward, it's a good idea to do a post CPR SUMA LOCK. This can be helpful in getting clear about what you might have done better and in soothing any leftover feelings that need to be discharged.

This resolution within one's self, to stay in the heart and endure whatever naturally arises, is the key to our own peace, and ultimately the key to peace on earth. If our experience of anger evolves, it will grow from an immature, misguided, destructive force to a mature and compassionate teaching response. Instead of trying to force changes in behavior, we align with the greater good and become masterful at appealing to the heart of our friend.

Communication in a relationship does not end when we part ways physically. Every thought we think and every feeling we feel toward each other affects the condition of the energetic container of the relationship. More often than not, conflicts are perpetuated by what we are thinking and feeling and how we say what we say when we finally say it. The *how* usually contains more *what* than what we actually think we are saying. How we say something extends from what we are being. And what we are being is an amalgamation of all the different thoughts and feelings leading up to any given moment. This is why awareness of feelings is so important—so we can be aware of what we are really doing and being and, in turn, what we are really saying.

The key to resolving these kinds of conflicts is the practice of courageous vulnerability and transparency, which begins in relationship with the self. Real resolution of conflict rarely means agreement. But it always means connection. It means seeing and being seen, and finding empathy even while we disagree. But before we can connect with others in this way, we have to connect with ourselves. We have to be completely honest with ourselves and accept ourselves for who we are. This is no easy feat. It is a life-long endeavor that is never finished. What is important is that we keep to the task and keep pace with the journey. Only then will we be ready and present and really capable of showing up in our relationships with others.

The Real Apology (FOR)

The root words of apology are "apo" and "logos." "Apo" means *away, of,* or *from.* "Logos" means *what we understand about our experience.* When we give an apology, we are giving by sharing what we have gathered from, of, or taken away from the experience. In other words, when we give an apology, we give what we understand about what happened or what we did. What reason does a friend have to trust again if we don't show new understanding of the conditions which lead to the original trespass? Without demonstrating that something has been learned from the experience, nothing has changed. Any expressed remorse or regret has very little substance, because the antici-pated behavior has not been addressed. To give an apology means we share what we have learned from our experience and we share it with feeling. It is intimate, honest, and vulnerable. We extend ourselves in an attempt to mend what we have broken and risk the pain of rejection as tribute to sincerity.

Set the intention. Affirm to yourself, "I am humble," "I am honest," "I really want to know my part in this trouble I experience," "I now allow myself to become aware of what is more and what could be better."

1. **Feel the feelings.** Allow the feelings of genuine remorse, regret, or guilt to pass through your being. In order for meaning to be arrived at, the discordant feelings must be fully felt. These are the feelings that let us know we have missed the mark, that we have acted in a way that is not true to who we really are or in accordance with how we want to be in the world. Again, our feelings are the messengers, so when we feel the feelings we are accepting the messages.

2. **Offer the apology.** Say, "I'm sorry." It's simple but it cannot really be done meaningfully without completing those initial feelings. Say "I'm sorry," and say it as you feel the feelings. Whatever the feelings are—sadness, guilt, remorse, regret, shame, hurt, fear, care, compassion, concern. Whatever's there, feel it when you say it. The feelings must be felt as the words are dealt, especially when apologizing. Otherwise the apology may seem contrived because the energy isn't moving.

3. **Repair what was broken.** Most often, what is broken is trust. In order to repair trust, we have to demonstrate that we have learned. This is the most important part of a real apology—to share what we have learned. Offering the apology communicates that you intend to make a change. But the substance of the thing is the change itself. We have to give our friend a plausible reason to begin reinvesting trust. We have to be able to envision and describe what we are going to do differently going forward. If we are feeling it and being it when we say it, our friend will know it.

There are times when it is not possible to apologize outside of the self. It may be that the trespass was so great that contact is refused or cannot be re-established. In either case we can still "take the meaning" from the experience and learn. We can feel our feelings about it and learn and decide what we will do differently going forward. In this way we can still honor the estranged relationship. In some rare cases it may be unhelpful to apologize outside of the self. If our friend's hurt child is activated and wildly projecting blame, an apology might compromise a needed boundary and actually hinder more than help. In such a case the apology could reinforce a friend's wounded conclusion that power and responsibility reside outside of the self. In any case, knowing when and how to apologize will always be a matter of feeling what feels right.

In truth, the real apology is FOR the self. It takes place within the self. When we do something we regret or feel guilt for, those feelings occur because we have acted outside of our personal integrity. We did something we didn't really want to do. Probably one of our old ego defense mechanisms, which is no longer serving us, got the best of us and we hurt someone. In most cases when we hurt someone, it is because we have in some way allowed neurotic fear to color our perception. We projected it outside of the self onto our friend, and we did or said something that hurt them. But the first betrayal or abandonment or separation that occurred was within the self, so we have to get right with ourselves. We have to slow down and feel the pain. We have to take the medicine, so we can see, "I apologize, first and foremost, for me."

Living Consciously in Integrity

As we become conscious in this way and learn to live in personal integrity, there is a beneficial impact warming everything we touch. We personally benefit by feeling happier and healthier as we move about in the world. We are becoming self-aware and more aware of what we personally contribute to the world, and we get busy doing it. Our fellow human beings benefit because we have empathy for them. We are able to feel what their experience is like and understand them. We are better equipped to address conflict and facilitate resolution, connection, and harmony. Our friends and family get to witness and interact with someone who is alive and awake and our every interaction with them inherently supports and points them to their own personal integrity. Even the earth benefits, because we become conscious of our relationship with her, have empathy for her, and make choices in all of our dealings to honor and care for her. When we meet our moment, lightning strikes through the nervous system and across the land. We lighten our individual burden and the collective burden of humanity. What we lift off the self removes just enough to make clearer and more hopeful the way for all.

*"One must marry one's feelings to one's beliefs and ideas.
That is probably the only way to achieve a measure of
harmony in one's life."*

−Napoleon Hill

How to Get Conscious

here is a container of subtle energy whirling within and around us that is our personal consciousness. The circulation and cycles of this energy are easily represented by the nervous, digestive, respiratory, and cardiovascular systems. Signals and substance are received in and sent out through the brain, belly, breath, and heart. All of this physical circulation in the body begins with, and is directed by, the condition of our consciousness. This is happening both immediately and chronically, over time. We are simultaneously experiencing what we can of the new and repeating what is left unfinished of the old. From the first beat of our embryonic heart to the present moment, every life experience we have gone through has contributed to the current condition of our brain, body, breath, heart, and our current state of consciousness—what we now experience as the self. It is possible to engage in conscious and deliberate somatic processes that heal and regulate what is unfinished or traumatized in the autonomic systems.

The Tuning Power of Chant

One particularly powerful healing somatic process is chanting. Repetition of any kind focuses the mind and has the power to reorganize, regulate, and heal the inhibited autonomic systems. Repetition of thought, word, and action concentrate and direct the subtle energy or feelings we experience as our consciousness. Great heights of inspiration and vision are easily attained with the chanting method of focused repetition. As humans, we instinctively know this truth. Without any training or encouragement, children can often be found chanting or singing something repetitive. Most religious traditions have practiced some form of chanting since their inception.

During chanting the mind is focused on a particular line of thought. The repetition ensures continued focus. As the mind stays attending to the chant, the autonomic systems begin to absorb and resend the feelings associated with its content. As our being is attuned by this method of focus, the surrounding environment becomes imbued as well. Iphelia serendipitously discovered her own chant and decided to share it. As the other children joined in the singing, the collective subtle energy became exponentially charged, sweeping across the countryside and into outer space.

We each have the capacity for empathy. We are all connected. When we find the courage to be whole and to share from our true heart, all benefit and all rejoice.

Make a Playlist (PLAY)

Feelings are vibration. Sound is vibration. Music is vibration. Repetitive vibration is powerful. Music is powerful. The qualities of the musical vibrations we listen to induce matching qualities of feeling. It is emotionally hygienic to be mindful and intentional about what we listen to, especially what we listen to repetitively.

Set your intention. Say out loud three times, "My feelings create my reality," "I choose how I want to feel as I feel my way to the reality I create," "I really want to feel more of what I want to create."

1. **Pick out your favorite feelings of all.** Become aware of how you want to feel in your life. Identify the feelings. Write them out. Put them in order of priority. What are the most important feelings for you to feel?

2. **List songs to match the feelings.** Make a playlist. Pick songs that feel the way you want to feel. Consider how each song resonates with you. If they have lyrics, what are the lyrics saying? Are they saying how you want to feel? How does the melody move you? How does the harmony of the different instruments move you?

3. **Aspire.** Keep your list with you and listen to it often. Sing along. Feel along! Allow yourself to resonate with the music and the meaning. As you listen and sing, imagine your life. Imagine your best self, your true self. Imagine expressing your true self in the world and what all that looks like. Visualize and sing and feel. As you reach new heights of inspiration, allow new thoughts and ideas to come that further support your path to creating the feeling-experience you seek. As you continue to grow, keep an ear out for new songs and feelings that you feel will help guide your way.

4. **Yay! Rejoice!** Move your body! Dance! Run! Kung Fu Fight! Just like your breath, your body's movement and posture is a revolving door following and forming feelings. Moving your body the way you want to feel causes those feelings to become more a part of your everyday being.

What we spend the majority of our time feeling deeply affects how we perceive and respond to everything in our world. Lyrics are thoughts. Thoughts generate feelings. Chanting an inspired affirmation generates inspired feelings. Singing along with heartbreak can be cathartic for a minute, but staying too long can keep us stuck. The songs we choose to listen to are magical incantations expressing powerful emotions through our being, which eventually crystallize into our life circumstances. Choose wisely.

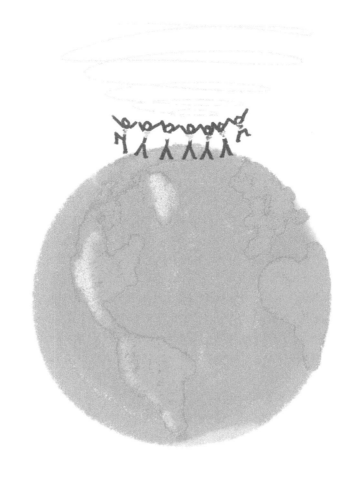

Meditate Meditate Meditate (SITTER)

Meditation is a powerful practice toward the endeavor of becoming ever more conscious. Whereas prayer and chanting are assertive actions of the mind and spirit, meditation is primarily a receptive action. Prayer is speaking. Meditation is listening.

There are innumerable types of meditation but always the process will involve a period where the mind is assertive, followed by a period where the mind is passive and receptive, receiving. In this way, the process of meditation enables one to focus and calm the mind and then experience the contrast between the ever-present, steady flow of unconditional love moving through the open heart and all the congested or unresolved feeling-energy that is in the way. Here is how Iphelia meditates:

Sit

Find or create a place that is comfortable and safe to turn within and withdraw from the senses for a while. Sit in this place with your spine straight. This allows all the subtle energies and feelings in the body to circulate optimally. Set the intention to open and expand your heart.

Inspire

Bring your attention to the present by focusing on the breath. Observe the breath. Notice the condition of the breath. Are there areas in your chest that are tight? Are there places in your breath cycle that feel difficult to reach? Breath is incredibly important. Breathing is feeling and feeling is breathing. How we feel is reflected in how we are breathing. When we stop breathing, we stop feeling. Begin regulating the breath toward a more balanced and rhythmic style of breathing. Let each breath reflect the same speed and rhythm as the preceding and proceeding breaths. When this kind of breathing is practiced and perfected, all the systems in the body become calm and balanced. The longer this mindful breath is maintained the more rooted in the present we become.

Tune

Attunement has already begun through regulating the breath. Now begin to use visualization to stimulate the opening heart. The universal archetype for awareness and goodwill is light. Imagine a light growing in your heart. With each breath the light becomes brighter and clearer. Feel a warmth in your heart, within the body and beyond the body. The light and warmth is strengthened by remembering all the love you have received in your life. It is strengthened also by feeling all the love you have to give to everyone in your life. Feelings of gratitude, compassion, acceptance, generosity, sincerity, love, care, and forgiveness all encourage the open heart.

Transmute

Address resistance to bring attention to the present. As the systems begin to calm, you will begin noticing thoughts and feelings that arise. Subjective Iphelia Moments may arise. Try to stay present with whatever arises. Visualize light and express open-hearted feeling toward and around the areas of consciousness causing discord. This will inevitably lead to the resolution of the issue in a positive way. It may come as an immediate flash of insight during the meditation. It may also come later as spontaneous insight or seemingly serendipitous events triggering new awarenesses. Always, the insight comes after core feelings have completed their natural cycle. Gradually, you'll feel the movement toward a more balanced state of being. Sometimes the process may be the healthy release of anger into a pillow, so that deeper, more vulnerable feelings can be accessed. Sometimes it may be the release of sadness. Sometimes it is atonement or visualization of the action we wish we'd have taken replacing the one we regret and resolving to do things differently in the future. Ultimately, it is a setting of things right within the self, a return to balance. As the figures of discord are addressed in this way, a growing appreciation for the present moment ensues. Heart-centered feelings begin to circulate, strengthening and vitalizing all the systems of the body. Eventually, there will become an energetic experience, or feeling, of the true self.

Expand

After bringing the self back to personal integrity, there is then the challenge of reaching and stretching for what is more. This can be done through visualizing light, love, and kindly feeling moving out from the heart in all directions toward all relations. Fill the room, the house, the surrounding community, the city, the whole country, the whole world, the universe. With the heart open, this practice of expansion permeates the physical environment with good energy, promotes harmonious relationships, increases self-awareness, and strengthens one's capacity for clean empathy.

Return

After sitting, meditation does not end. The challenge is to stay conscious and aware as we walk in the world. Slowly bring the attention back to the body, staying in balance, keeping the heart open. After rising, stay present with the feelings. Notice the contrast of feelings that different thoughts and actions inspire. This is your inner guidance. This is the real practice, staying conscious of our relationship with the self as we think and speak and act in the world. Aligning the self with what feels right and good and true. Inevitably, the extended body of your life circumstances begins to change and strengthen and support living in personal integrity.

Meditation Pro Tips

- Establish a consistent space to meditate. It should be a conscious space. Put sacred objects in that space which remind you to be conscious. Things you are grateful for and things that open your heart when you see them. This space will become imbued with the feeling-energy you practice radiating when you are there and will support you in getting conscious when you return to the space.

- Always come back to the breath. Breathing is feeling, feeling is breathing. If you are having trouble dropping into a meditative state of mind, just focus on the breath, regulate the breath. Eventually your focus and state of mind will improve.

- Keep the faith. If you start your meditation practice and things in your life become more difficult or you start to feel more emotional, do not dismay. It means you are catching up on unfinished business! Be easy on yourself, believe in yourself, and strive to have compassion toward yourself. Have faith in the process. Relief is on the horizon.

- Fight the good fight. Remember that no effort is ever a waste. When you are struggling to manage your state, struggling to concentrate, or slowing down leads you to feeling down, know that these are the times when you are building courage and fortitude. Stick with it. Finish what is unfinished.

- Sit with will and intent. Everything you think and feel in the realm of your own consciousness has an impact on how you will feel and what you will experience when you stand up and move about your day. Meditation is not daydreaming. It is house-cleaning. Set your intentions and will your state straight. Use this sacred time wisely.

"The more often he feels without acting, the less he will be ever to act, and, in the long run, the less he will be able to feel..."

–C. S. Lewis

The Continuum of Feeling (COF)

Becoming conscious can be challenging. Our old defense mechanisms are constantly at work keeping us safe—keeping us from feeling our feelings. Some of us might tell ourselves we are more conscious than we actually are. Some of us may believe we are less conscious than we actually are. Grandiosity and self-doubt are both forms of defense. For those wanting to experience more and willing to apply radical self-honesty, the following model is useful for plotting a course.

This is a continuum of feeling-experience. At one end are those of us who are completely cut off from feeling. At the other end are those who live constantly aware of an additional dimension of experience in their life.

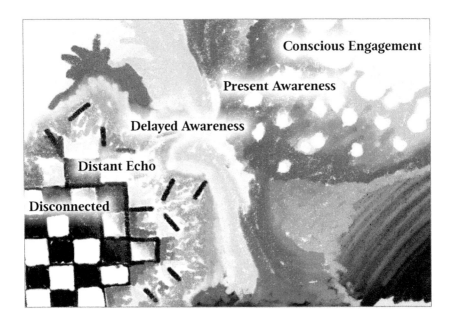

Disconnected (Never Feeling)

The disconnected individual is unconscious of the defense mechanisms that automatically strive to avoid feeling any feelings of joy or pain. Joy is avoided because it is too risky to loosen the lid on any feeling for fear of the pain that could arise. This individual lives life mostly in thought and is usually quite disconnected from the body or overly identified with the body and its senses. There is no real connection with self and thus no real experience of connection with friends and family. The likelihood of a chemical addiction of some kind is very high, though use may be extremely normalized and abuse unacknowledged. Here, empathy is not possible. The individual may express *sympathy* toward another, but this will be the result of what has mostly been identified via the reproduction of an experience in thought.

Distant Echo (Sometimes Feeling)

Some of us experience feelings like echoes of our inner life. When we do not give due attention to our inner life, we dim the line of communication between our conscious self and our true self. We exist in life but are not living fully. We slow the growth of self-awareness, sometimes tragically to a full stop. We find ways to treat our angst with process addictions or even chemical addictions. We have appreciation for insights that come, but we are not able to maintain a steady connection with that inspired part of ourselves. We live frustrated, ignorant of the connection between our stifled spirit and our pattern of avoidance and repression of our deeper unfinished feelings.

Delayed Awareness (Healing Begins)

The awareness of feeling is awakened, but delayed. We have hit our bottom in some way and discovered some kind of peace after the storm, which has tuned us in to the importance of allowing the natural cycle of emotion. Here we become interested in the experience of feeling, but do not yet have immediate access to or understanding of what is happening when it happens. We are in transition. We tend to realize our experience through hindsight. Something happens and we feel angry or hide, usually act in a regrettable way, and later recognize we were guarding against some deeper, more vulnerable feeling. This is the stage where feelings or experiences that were left incomplete from the past may resurface, sometimes as memory but often as reactions to present circumstances that somehow resemble the incomplete past. Delayed awareness is the stage most us live in. We struggle with our relationships because we struggle in our relationship with the self. We long for connection or medicate the longing away. All the while real connection and real medicine lie within.

After enough contemplation and failed experience, we realize the power and importance of staying present with what we are feeling. Once we have thought about it enough and gathered enough subjective evidence, we start making a consistent effort and begin to recognize feelings as they are happening.

Present Awareness (Often Feeling)

Here we have learned to maintain a fairly constant practice of observing what we experience emotionally. As a result, a gradually increasing self-awareness ensues and healing begins to take a steady course. We have turned the corner. Feelings are appreciated and embraced. We are conscious of our need to deal with our feelings and choose to take time to slow down and connect with ourselves. We are conscious of our individual addictive tendencies. We appreciate how much richer and fuller our experience of life is when we are fully tapped into our emotions. We choose to exercise restraint toward our chemical and process avoidance patterns. We begin exercising discernment with our choices. When we feel our emotions becoming too crowded or congested we recognize it and course-correct. We begin to organize our life around what feels most natural and balanced to the self. Eventually, through consistent attention to our feelings, the inherent need for personal integrity becomes visible to us and we begin sculpting the boundaries of our life to be something that allows greater expression for our true self.

Conscious Engagement (Always Feeling)

When an individual is primarily living in the present, fully aware of what she is experiencing emotionally or energetically, she is consciously engaged. The individual comes to realize the inescapable truth that she is fully connected to everything and everyone around her. She cannot help but recognize that her thoughts and feelings are constantly touching and being touched by everything that occurs in her consciousness. This becomes true not only for what is apparent in the material circumstances of her daily living, but also what, at any given moment, she inwardly shines the light of her attention on—beyond time and space!

Here, the individual has prioritized her personal integrity and sees very clearly the connection between self care and any real care that could be offered to those around her. She has set firm boundaries with any forces that would compromise her. Her life circumstances have taken a form that support her in being whole and contained, and allow her ever-increasing opportunities for creative expression of her true self, her true purpose in life. This supports the same in everyone around her.

The COF is a personal tool for measuring progress and planning how we can improve. For each individual there may be areas of consciousness where more or less awareness of feeling occurs. Areas related to a particular brand of abuse may make feelings more difficult to discern for someone who has a similar history in need of healing. A man who had an abusive father might be more aware of his feelings when in the company of women. A woman who had an emotionally unstable mother might choose to repress her feelings of vulnerability in an effort to avoid being like her mother, without seeing that her pattern of suppression leads to explosions which very much resemble the behavior she is trying to avoid. There are infinite scenarios. Each path to awakening runs through a unique forest with varying shadows. As we progress, we cycle through light and dark, through periods of intense difficulty and graceful ease. Our place on the continuum is not stable. We vacillate up and down as we grapple with our healing and awakening. Our progress is filled with regressions as new baselines are established. Let our striving endure, beset with gentle care and compassion toward ourselves and each other.

How to Feel Your Feelings

Most of us have unknowingly learned to repress our feelings. We unconsciously avoid feelings of discomfort and find ways to distract and suppress ourselves. Any one of the various methods of suppression can become so ingrained that we think the defense mechanisms are actually the bounds of reality, the actual parameters and limits to our life experience. Anything emerging outside of those limitations is then viewed as false, dysfunctional, or even a threat. This is the briefest description of the problem. A more in-depth understanding can be gained by exploring the solution.

- Seek your neurochemical baseline. Whatever the mind altering substances you use, refrain. Ensure that periods of sobriety are built into your lifestyle. Make commitments to yourself to lengthen those periods. If you find this challenge too daunting, get help.

- Identify and address process addictions. Strive to be conscious of the ways you avoid your feelings and instead practice staying present.

- Turn off external sensory stimulation devices. Phones, computers, gaming consoles, SCREENS. They're everywhere! These powerful tools can be used to connect or disconnect from your feelings, depending on the content and your intention for using them. At worst, they become process addictions that can keep us distracted from the good work of improving our relationships, enhancing our life circumstances, and discovering our life's purpose. At best, we make them mediums of connection and creativity that empower and inspire us into action. We have to be really honest to know, but always, the surest method for getting in touch with our feelings is to reduce stimulation.

- Breathe, take deep breaths. Our breath is intrinsically connected to our feelings. Our feelings are the breath of our souls. Breathing is feeling and feeling is breathing. Watch a person who is about to cry but doesn't want to show vulnerability. Invariably, they will hold their breath. When we stop the physical breath or breathe shallow, we stop feeling our soul, we stop the breath of life. Everything becomes dim and lifeless. The condition of our breath mirrors how we experience life. Breathe fully and live fully.

- Seek the beautiful silence. All sensory input is based on contrast. To perceive a clear impression of what is happening within, our best point of contrast is inner silence or stillness. This doesn't mean that we always achieve silence, but the striving for it keeps us growing more deeply and acutely aware of what is happening in our inner life.

- Make time to listen within. Make time to connect with yourself. Establish a routine. Conscious and deliberate efforts are essential to overcome the habits of repression. Meditate. Meditate. Meditate.

211

- Spend time in nature. Nature is a bridge between our worldly life experience and a deeper connected soul experience. Everything in nature is empathic. Everything is tuned in to everything else and everything is cooperating. If we pay attention and listen with feeling, we discover that nature is constantly communicating to us through synchronicity and omen. Just being in nature for any length of time is a powerful healing experience.

- Create and maintain relationships that are truly intimate. Seek friendships and community with others who can offer clean empathy. There is nothing more conducive to finishing unfinished feelings than choosing to share and being witnessed by a true friend or friends.

*"The intuitive mind is a sacred gift
and the rational mind is a faithful servant.
We have created a society that honors the servant
and has forgotten the gift."*

–Albert Einstein

Awakening
The Gift of Feeling

 here is an invisible energetic realm that resides just behind the physical one we appear to live in. As we become conscious, we wake up to this world. Just as we are now conscious of what we are wearing, we develop a constant awareness of what we are being in thought and feeling. Breaks in our personal integrity create unsightly holes in our spirit's clothing, allowing unwanted conditions to enter in. Each feeling lends its voice to our appearance. Erroneous judgments of inferiority or superiority make for soil and stench. Shame can be an awful stain that takes time and attention to remove. And joy radiates cleansing and renewing light toward all surrounding. Everything has consciousness and feeling and everything and everyone is connected.

When heaven descends on earth it will not come from the sky. It will come through the hearts of courageous women and men. Women and men who choose to be still and breathe and feel. Radically honest women and men who dare to face and endure their discomfort and heed its many messages. Women and men who quest inward time and again to discover what they are not and distill the truth of who they really are. Empathic women and men who choose to keep their heart's eye open, step through to the eye of their own inner storm, and find peace. Women and men awakening the gift of feeling.

215

"Aho Mitakuye Oyasin. We are all related."

–Lakota Sioux Prayer

Awakening Community

At this time on the planet, most communities relate in a way that is gener-ally callous and sarcastic. The callous protects and the sarcasm masks the attacking behaviors that perpetuate the callous. We tease and compete and posture and perform. We dodge and parry to stay safe and dance to win love. The driving feeling behind all this behavior is fear. We unconsciously fear our inferiority, so we silently judge others to compensate. We project our fear of being judged because we are being judgmental. Instead of looking inward and gathering real self worth by adhering to our hearts, we look out and compare and compete. It is a harsh and lonesome reality, passed down through the ages, that most of us have become used to. Relating in this way has created a world where disconnection and the resulting pressurized aggression seem like a normal way of life. We have become insensitive to ourselves and each other and insensitive to the environment, our home, the earth.

Within every action and every object is an invisible energetic structure that reflects the conditions of consciousness that created it. No matter what the appearance is, sooner or later the real condition of its inner structure becomes visible in the world. This is why, when operating from neurotic fear, we can-not help but create more problems to fear. The collective, impatient need to travel faster and farther through the burning of fossil fuels has caused us the experience of running out of time. The fear of being alone seeks superficial compromise that distorts and distracts from real intimacy. The fear of paying too much purchases an inferior product that soon needs a more expensive replacement. The fear of not having enough drives us to work ourselves so hard that we eventually lose our health and die, without ever enjoying what we have. Everywhere neurotic fear is active there is this tragic and paradoxi-cal end. Neurotic fear shortens our breath and shortens our sight.

Everything that hurts, all of the atrocities in the world, all of them, extend from our collective emotional repression. When we repress our emotions, we repress our awareness of the truth. Our vision becomes short-sighted. We don't consider the long-term outcomes of our choices because we don't feel the warnings from the larger part of ourselves. We lose touch with our conscience and we act without wisdom. We unconsciously make choices guided by fear, and we suffocate our spirit. Our character devolves as the old lizard brain takes hold. We fight, becoming angry, defensive, inconsiderate, and selfish. Or we run away and hide via avoidance and addiction.

There is another way...

Become a Dragon!

Moment by moment, walk in the world, observing your inner life and caring for it. Finish feelings. Honor your sadness. Allow your joy. Allow glee! Get the messages. Put the anger where it goes! Meditate. Stay conscious. Live true to your heart. Find gratitude. Avoid avoidance. Avoid addiction. Face fear. Introspect. Shore up your bowl. Maintain integrity. Strengthen up your mature adult. Love on your connected kid. Meditate. Release projections. Release judgment. Speak the truth. Express authentically. Walk tall. Breathe fully. Be the thing. With your every breath, be a contradiction to false constructs, egoism, and narcissism. Meditate. Release shame. Radiate love. Be humble and courageous—vulnerable and strong. Set healthy boundaries. Make real apologies. Clean it up. Guard the sensitivity in the self and protect sensitivity in others. Show up. Clear assumptions, ask for what you want, say what you will do. And do it!

Moment by moment we can reshape our world. When we live true to our hearts, fear no longer blinds our way. Courage guides our way. Everything we do contributes to creations that are clean and shiny and lasting. Our thoughts and feelings generate spectacular crystalline structures that seed unique qualities of peace and beauty and cooperation in the world. Eventually, our individual efforts yield a critical mass effect. Instead of sarcastic bites, communities begin to interact with genuine care and kindly feeling. Instead of judgment, empathy and compassion flow between us. Eventually, our collective heart-centered feelings condense and the emotional atmosphere we live and breathe in is transformed. Pervasive feelings of support, abundance, and connection circulate throughout all the lands. Instead of feeling separate and lonely we all come to know, through feeling, that we are one.

Moment by moment, when we resolve to release our projections and become what we want to see, we make the ultimate contribution to our community, humanity.

The Dragon Heart

The subconscious mind often communicates to the conscious mind through symbols. This can happen through dreams or synchronistic events we notice throughout our day. We may even notice symbols that grab our attention through the scenery of our lives, such as a child's drawing.

Iphelia's purple dragon heart possesses both the passionate power of red and the placid peace of blue—it embodies an integration of the two. It represents the courage to feel and embrace all of the self, beginning with the parts that are most detrimental to avoid, like fear and anger. It represents facing fear and transforming blame and anger into healthy personal power. It represents the evolution of human character through the effort to consciously transmute one's old lizard brain responses. Instead of reacting from fear or old defense mechanisms and secondary anger, we observe ourselves, we feel where we really are, and we face our fears. We practice staying conscious and present and our inner workings slow down. The old brain response of fight or flight is not so quick to consume us and new choices are made. We finish what is unfinished and aspire to reach an ever-better-feeling place. What once held us down, crawling low to the ground, has grown wings and evolved and now empowers the heart to fly. We show up, meet our moment, and demonstrate the ferocity of a giant-hearted, fire-breathing, purple dragon!

Becoming a GHFBPD

The reptilian brain is ancient. It is where our base emotional energy is first processed. Those base emotions drive us to survive. Feelings like fear and rage and the urge to merge and procreate! The archetype of the dragon represents the power and mystery of those drives. Throughout the history of the world dragons have represented extremes of intensity. In the West they have represented the ego, overindulgence, temptation, and monstrous obstacles to be overcome. The dragons of the East, particularly those of the Orient, have represented primordial forces of nature, spiritual power, wisdom, and even divinity. For Iphelia, dragons are a symbol of integration. A mythical creature native to earth, water, wind, and fire. They embody darkness and light, passion and peace. They are a symbol of freedom, autonomy, and wholeness.

Becoming a dragon means learning to value sensitivity, authenticity, and integrity. It means aspiring to show up in life and live true to one's heart. In essence, allowing one's self to fully feel and trust one's feelings.

Feelings are our fire. Fire transforms everything it touches. A deadly, destructive force or a powerful energy source, it can cause incredible explosions when suppressed. If not allowed to breathe, it smolders cold to lifeless ash and dust. When tended to with care and containment, our feelings provide warmth, like the fire that sustains us through winter. Fire has always been, and is still, our light in darkness.

Dragons breathe fire. Breathing fire is breathing fully, feeling all our feelings and caring for them. As human beings, we feel our fire burning just beneath the heart, at our core. To stay alive, we have to breathe, because the fire fueling the heart needs air. Feeling our feelings is allowing air to reach the source of fire within the heart. Feeling our feelings can at times be very uncomfortable, but it keeps us alive and awake and aware. Dragons live by this truth.

Dragons are old and wise. They feel and heed the messages of their emotions. They mature and grow wise because they maintain communication with the deeper, wiser part of themselves through feeling.

Dragons are deeply connected to mother earth. They maintain a conscious and personal relationship with her. They always remember that she is their mother and they are a living part of her. For dragons this is easy to remember because they allow themselves to feel their feelings. Their sensitivity gives them constant awareness of this fact, because they can feel it.

Dragons are fierce and courageous. They speak their truth, even when they are afraid. They know that every opportunity to face their fear stokes the fire within. And they know if their fire smolders it could mean going to sleep for years or even decades, until they awaken and live free again.

Dragons are humble. They know their place in the context of life. They know they belong to the earth. They know that they came from the earth and one day they will return to the earth. They know they are never superior or inferior, but that all have equal value, all are reducible to ash.

Dragons are considerate. Wherever they are, they know how to cooperate with the ecosystem around them and they do so for the sake of the highest good for all concerned.

Dragons are honest. They know that everything changes and everything dies, and this is their secret to longevity. When they feel that something within them is no longer serving them, or is hurting themselves and others, they look right at it. They feel it, breathe with it, using it as fuel for their inner fire, which energizes them to determine a new way. What once existed as shame or guilt or blame is transformed into treasures of honor and commitment to the self and the world.

Dragons are free. They can fly. They go wherever they want and do what they want. They don't make agreements they know they can't keep and they don't ask for promises. They want everyone to be free. They don't pretend to be more than they are. They don't reduce themselves to be less. They aspire to be present and to be the same self wherever they go.

Dragons are strong. They have impeccable self-respect and they always stand up for themselves. They know that by respecting and honoring themselves at every turn, they are, in turn, supporting everyone else in the same. They know all are worthy and all belong.

Dragons are magical. They are extraordinarily creative. They are able to conjure powerful feelings of inspiration, which they use to materialize all of their hearts' desires into the world.

Dragons are perceptive. They see the unseen. They can see far into the probable future and deep into the etiological past. They use their feelings to look within and sense the real conditions of their inner life, and to look out into their world and sense what is within those before them and what is likely to happen next. They use this power to guard their mother and serve the highest good of all.

Dragons are practical but they don't get bogged down by too many details. They know there is simply too much information in the world to process completely. So they mind their own business and trust that they can navigate complexity with a more advanced form of intelligence: feeling. They know when they feel right with themselves they can detect the contrast between what they are being (what they know themselves to be and like being) and what they feel before them. Then, without having to know every detail, they can make healthy discerning choices for themselves, their communities, and the earth.

Dragons are whole. They know that they have within them the capacity to be all the things they perceive outside of themselves and therefore refrain from judging others.

Dragons are fire keepers. They are conscious of the terrible force of aggression that is always burning inside of them and they are ever watchful within to ensure they not express it in a harmful way.

Dragons are not exhibitionists. They spend most of their time in the forest acting behind the scenes. They do not seek attention to feed their own vanity or grandiosity. Instead they perform for their own inner audience. They continually aspire to win the applause of their higher self by adhering to the silent instruction of their wise inner knowing, their conscience.

Dragons know the difference between healthy fear and neurotic fear. They remember to take time to attune themselves to their mother, the earth. Their sensitivity allows them to feel her, always there, always protecting and providing for all their needs. Allowing themselves to feel real connection and support enables them to discern what is healthy fear from what is neurotic fear.

Dragons are individual. The most important relationship in their lives is the relationship they keep with their own conscience. They know that being faithful and adherent to their own inner guidance is what empowers them to wield their fire in the world.

At one end of the continuum of human feeling are those of us who live our lives constantly trying to extinguish fires. By avoiding our feelings, we avoid ourselves; we avoid speaking, avoid listening, avoid confrontation and real connection. Some of us spend our lives motivated by fear. Fear of not having enough or being enough, fear of judgment or abandonment, fear of overwhelm or perhaps the most powerful fear of all: death! As a result, we continually unconsciously recreate circumstances that contain opportunities to face these fearsome fires and run in circles trying to put them out!

At the other end are those who breathe fire. They allow their feelings. They are awake and aware and actively creating in their lives. For these individuals, fire is something they embrace and channel. Feelings of hurt and sadness and fear ignite transformational fires within that they use to breathe fires of inspiration into the world. Instead of running from life, these individuals are feverishly in pursuit of life. Instead of being driven by fear and avoidance, they persevere and create their vision.

Become a dragon. Breathe your fire. Allow it to transform you. Then breathe into the world and make your contribution.

Feeling Awareness, A New Paradigm

1. Feelings are real.

2. Feelings are everywhere.

3. Feelings are messages from the self and others.

4. Feelings tell us who we are and what we prefer.

5. Feelings tell us what we are really being and what our real intentions are.

6. Feelings give us valuable information about everything we place our attention on.

7. Feeling words are symbols that describe conditions in consciousness.

8. Feeling words help us to stay conscious and help us communicate our experience.

9. *Empathy* is the universal phenomenon whereby, through placing our attention on another person, we experience the same or similar feelings as they are experiencing.

10. *Projection* is the universal phenomenon whereby old unconscious wounds are attributed to current circumstances that resemble the past.

11. *Clean Empathy* is accurate, free of projection, and makes no assumptions. It supports others in identifying their own feelings and coming to their own insights.

12. *Personal Empathy* is having empathy for the self by allowing and observing the natural cycle of emotion.

13. Discovering and knowing one's *true self* is not possible without the practice of personal empathy.

14. When we ignore or suppress feelings, we deny potential self-awareness and lessen our capacity for empathy.

15. When we allow and observe the natural cycle of emotion, we increase our self-awareness and increase our capacity for empathy.

16. A fundamental feeling of growing stability that results from thinking and acting in accordance with what feels right and good and true in our heart comes with personal empathy.

17. *Personal Integrity* is our ability to consistently heed the heart's feeling-guidance with little or no compromise, which results in genuine self-awareness and an authentic expression of our true self in the world.

18. Clean empathy is only possible when we have conscious awareness of personal integrity.

19. Striving to accept total responsibility for the self is essential for achieving clean empathy and personal integrity.

20. Virtuous acts of goodwill which benefit humanity all extend from personal integrity.

21. Worldly integrity is not possible without personal integrity.

22. All forms of addiction, egocentric neurosis, and narcissism result from and perpetuate suppressed feeling-energy.

23. Choosing to stay conscious and feel feelings requires courage and fortitude.

24. *Humility* is a balanced state of being that results from the practice of courage and fortitude required to stay conscious.

25. The *Iphelia Moment* is any moment in time when we become conscious of the choice to move toward or away from connection with and expression of our true self in the world.

26. Living free of repression and addiction and allowing and observing the natural cycle of emotion eventually makes us more sensitive, self-aware, and perceptive.

27. Increasing self-awareness eventually leads to conscious management of the relationship between three distinct parts of the self: *The Child, The Mature Adult,* and *The Higher Self.*

28. When these three parts of the self are connected our character evolves beyond old reactive defense mechanisms to a greater capacity for consciously managing feeling-energy.

29. Our capacity for conscious management of our own feeling-energy is real maturity and empowers us with the capacity for personal empathy, personal integrity, and clean empathy for all with whom we come into contact.

30. Getting conscious and staying conscious of feeling awareness requires practice.

31. There are various methods of practice for staying conscious, including chanting, meditation, introspection, and contemplation.

32. The healing we achieve within the self benefits our friends, our families, our communities, and the earth.

33. The development of feeling awareness and the practice of empathy is imperative to the survival of humanity.

Empathy Knows Glossary (EKG)

eeling words represent symbols that point toward common energy patterns of various intensities and durations. Each of us adopts unique and different symbols for feeling words. This can be demonstrated by a simple exercise in free association. One person's symbol may actually be the memory of an earlier life experience, another's may be a visualized personal creation, a sound, a body memory, or even a conglomeration of other experiences or intellectual concepts. This is all determined by what we have gathered and created along the way. When we hear the word, it is the symbol that brings us to our relationship with that common experience and our present understanding of it. The purpose of this glossary is to assist with gathering and promoting a deeper understanding of the universal processes of feeling we all experience.

Abandoned The experience of an unexpected loss of connection that was once relied on. A combination of sadness about loss of connection, hurt over broken trust, and fear of how to be without what was lost.

Afraid The experience of fear in the form of worry. Something bad is going to happen or something good will not happen. See Fear, page 128.

Anger The experience of concentrated intensity of emotion always intending to cause change or control outcome. Healthy anger sets boundaries and restores power. Unhealthy anger causes emotional congestion and harm. See Anger, page 123.

Ashamed The experience of dissociation from the true self as a result of identification with outside projections. See also Shame, page 240.

Amused The experience of joy through giving attention to something reflecting a beautiful aspect of self, which is either familiar and dear to us, or that we desire to be more connected with.

Assertive The experience of certainty and empowerment. Feeling right and doing something with it.

Awe The experience of witnessing something that immediately, and at times involuntarily, triggers the opening of the heart. There is profound gratitude for what is beheld, beyond self interest.

Blame The experience of anger rising to compensate for and avoid the more vulnerable experience of responsibility and sadness, hurt, or fear.

Bored The experience of loss resulting from fixating on the future because of a perceived need for external stimulation. A common symptom of addictive patterns.

Calm The experience of a quieting of the usual feeling patterns. A feeling of space opens up, usually after having released some degree of congestion or distancing in perspective, such as attuning to nature or meditation.

Caring The experience of empathy toward a perceived need outside of the self. Feeling compelled to help. Healthy when directed to a real opportunity to support another in their own sincere effort. Unhealthy when coming from the projection of one's own unaddressed need onto another who isn't really seeking help or is not sincere in their own effort.

Compassion The experience of empathy paired with love and caring. Healthy when the person receiving compassion cares for himself and feels real gratitude for the love and care he is given. Unhealthy when the empath cares more than the receiving person and is taken advantage of or feels drained by the experience. Healthy compassion generates more energy. Unhealthy compassion quickly depletes energy and rather than really help, enables unhealthy patterns. When we recognize unhealthy codependent patterns, setting boundaries is a compassionate and empowering response for everyone involved.

Confident The experience of connection and support generating trust and momentum for an endeavor. Acting from a state of personal integrity.

Confused The experience of a mental fog or chaos, resulting from immense and/or prolonged emotional congestion, which has depleted mental resources of attention and memory, rendering the feeler unable to accurately perceive and find meaning in their experience.

231

Content The experience of completion of a cycle of emotion. There is space in-between the movements. There is satisfaction and peace.

Creative The experience of the open heart converging with the active mind. Expansive feelings reveal new visions and new ideas.

Depressed The experience of a loss of energy, hope, and sight of what could be resulting from a prolonged lack of creative expression for the true self. Usually brought on by an identification with experiences which started the repression, creating a very stiflingly false or limited self-concept and/or world view. Healthy depression allows the system a period of withdrawal or deep rest, which would allow the investment in the false self-concept or world view to relax, while hope or sight of what could be returns. Unhealthy when the individual is unable to withdraw and the congestive constructs are not allowed to relax and weaken, which compounds the congestion further. This compounding of congestion can eventually lead to a loss of the will to live.

Desperate The experience of acting on behalf of fear in an attempt to obtain something one believes one cannot live without or avoid something one believes one cannot live with.

Disappointment The experience of the heart releasing what was hoped for or expected. Mild or low-grade sadness.

Disgust The experience of anger paired with shame. Denial of some part of the self projected onto others, or secondary anger focused towards the self for the purpose of suppressing very much feared immense grief. Disgust is the result of unacknowledged shame and the sadness that could release it.

Doubtful The experience of mild secondary anger focused on the future for the purpose of suppressing the fear of something good not happening.

Embarrassed The experience of hurt and/or sadness coupled with fear resulting from the perceived judgments of others.

Excited The experience of energy gathering in the body resulting from anticipation for something sought for or the potential for something to begin. The emotional body is preparing to move a lot of energy.

Fear The experience of descending into darkness, a loss of self. The experience of fear offers contrast to love and safety. Healthy fear is a warning. It draws contrast that allows for discernment toward a desired outcome. Unhealthy fear is neurotic fear of what is not really there. Neurotic fear is a constant vacuum that is projected outside of the self. Usually caused by unfinished feelings from the past projected on to current circumstances. Ultimately the only way to become free of neurotic fear is to find a way to face it. See Fear, page 128.

Free The experience of the open heart allowing full expression of the true self.

Frightened The experience of fear in the form of anticipating an interruption of safety. See also Startled.

Frustration The experience of mild or low-grade anger hanging on, attempting to resist an undesired outcome over which one has no control.

Generous The experience of the open heart, full and overflowing with gratitude. The natural desire to share and give when the heart is open and full.

Glad The experience of gratitude resulting from fulfillment and/or relief.

Glee The experience of the open heart, full and free. A peak experience of gratitude for freedom of expression of the true self.

Grateful The experience of seeing through the open heart. Seeing the truth. Breathing through the heart, receiving and giving simultaneously. See Gratitude, page 134.

Guilt The experience of sadness resulting from acting out of alignment with the heart or true self. Doing something we really don't want to do. There is a need to return, atone, and/or reconnect with the true self. We hurt the self. Healthy guilt is some-

times experienced after causing harm to another person, but it is indicating harm to the self and is a healthy alarm informing us that we are off-track. Unhealthy guilt is feeling guilty for something for which we are not really responsible. In this case, it is a projection of personal guilt over not being true to the self. If it remains unconscious, this pattern can perpetuate itself and compound feelings of guilt, ultimately leading to a chronic experience of guilt or shame.

Happy The experience of the true self getting full expression in the world. Convergence of the experience of the true self and the circumstances in one's life. There is harmony.

Hate The experience of identification with pain resulting from extremely intense loss that has never been released, or from the build-up of unexpressed loss repressed over time. The heart is closed. The feeler is separated from the self and from what is being perceived. Empathy is not possible in this state.

Hope The experience of energy and enthusiasm in response to awareness of what could be that is in alignment with the true self.

Hurt The experience of pain in the heart due to a structure we have invested in such as an ideal, a hope, an agreement, or a connection or trust being broken. Hurt is usually followed by sadness and grief for what was lost.

Innocent The experience of subjective lightness and freedom resulting from choosing to live without secrets or the need to control another person. Acceptance of the past and the sincere intent to live ever more true to self in the present, with nothing to hide and no shame.

Jealousy The experience of fear of not having our heart's desire projected outside the self. The pain of unfulfilled dreams or desires is blamed on another. Rather than challenging the self and facing fear within the self, focusing on what another has. A need to create one's own desires for one's self.

Joy The experience of fulfillment after a period of loss or lack. The heart is filled, overflowing, feeling abundant, feeling whole. See Joy, page 132.

Kind The experience of genuine good will toward others. The heart is open, grateful, and generous.

Lonely The experience of a disconnect from self and/or others. Separation from the self occurs when we act in a way that is not true to the self. Connection with the self allows for real connection with others. Disconnection from the self renders our interactions  superficial. One can feel lonely while with other people, or feel content and connected while alone.

Love The experience of feeling-energy that is always present radiating from the open heart. We some- times lose sight of it, but it is always there, a con- stant expanding and inclusive feeling. Healthy love supports greater expression of one's heart or true self  and promotes connection, allowing for real empathy. Unhealthy love is not really love but emotional attachment used to avoid facing fear and/or sad- ness. Unhealthy love is fear, mistaken as love. See Love, page 133.

Mad The experience of operating from a state of anger. See also Anger, page 229.

Mean The experience of giving anger expression with projection. In other words, we attack. Rec- ognizing we feel mean is usually accompanied by a healthy dose of guilt. There is anger and blame, but there is also empathy. Recognition of the destructive  futility of avoidance through projection has to some degree begun.

Nervous The experience of energy and intensity gathering in the body resulting from anticipation of something new, unexpected, or potentially undesir- able about to happen.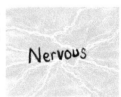

Peace The experience of stillness without emotional congestion. After being present with the self long enough the system is all caught up and can there- fore flow at its natural pace. Between each inhale and exhale there is a space. In that space we can be  fully present with the self. The practice of releasing emotional congestion is paradoxically conducive to experiencing more peace in one's life.

Proud The experience of acknowledging accom- plishment. Healthy pride is the resulting effect of achieving some measure of personal integrity. Unhealthy pride compensates for and hides shame or inferiority by telling the self and/or others a story and projecting a false sense of self.

Pure The experience of honest acceptance and non- judgment toward the self and others. Listening to, and acting from, the true self. A state of balance.

Rejected The experience of hurt resulting from an unmet hope or expectation of connection.

Resentment The experience of congested pain and anger, not yet given meaningful expression. Anger is held onto because of the belief that one is  powerless. There is a need to meet an external force with an equal and balancing force from within the self. Once a boundary has been truly set, the resentment will release.

Right The experience of increased energy resulting from acting in alignment with the true self.

Sad The experience of the heart releasing. Sadness is about loss, something torn from the heart. Feelings of sadness must be completed or fully released to make room for what is new. See Sadness, page 130.

Safe The experience of feeling supported in being one's true self. We seek to live in integrity while being surrounded by those who also seek to live in integrity. No secrets are kept, no boogeyman hides in the closet. Trust, which allows for real relaxation and the natural expression of the self, exists, and with it, peace.

Secure The experience of stability, connection, and trust. There is healthy attachment to something or someone trustworthy.

Self-Assured The experience of strength derived from the repeated expression of positive thoughts and feelings toward and from the self. Connection and support are felt from the self. Through being true to the self, we find real and lasting confidence.

Shame The experience of repressed sadness or grief about the self. We have identified with a message about the self that is not true or with a period of misalignment from the heart or true self. The belief that "I am bad," rather than, "I did something bad,"  or "Something bad happened to me." When identification with the false message is recognized, the sadness can then be allowed to move and the shame can finally be released. Shame is always a lie. We are never broken or bad. We have only ever, for a time, lost our way.

Sharing The experience of connection and love resulting from following the natural impulse of the open heart to give and receive.

Startled The experience of a sudden, unexpected experience that interrupts safety. See also Frightened.

Stressed The experience of suppressing the natural flow of emotion and attempting to focus attention elsewhere.

Strong The experience of life force filling the body and awakening the mind resulting from acting in alignment with the true self. A state of personal integrity.

Surprised The experience of a sudden unexpected jolt to the system. We experience surprise in different ways, depending on what is already circulating in the system. For example: Someone with a lot of secrets may experience surprise as shocking and  accompanied by a lot of fear. Someone without all those repressed feelings might experience surprise with hope and excitement.

Tired The experience of a depletion of emotional and/or physical energy due to compromise or imbalance, usually beginning as emotional congestion of some kind. Acting out of alignment with the true self  because of avoidance or neurotic fear, which quickly drains the system.

Trust The experience of a strong and stable connection which comes from knowing another is aware of you and sees you and supports you by advocating on behalf of your best interest in thought and feeling  and action. There is safety and security.

Weak The experience of a depletion in physical or emotional energy, which began due to a compromise in personal integrity.

Weary The experience of depletion of emotional energy due to personal compromise or need for improved boundaries. Noticing one is out of alignment before the compromise has progressed to the point of becoming physically tired.

Worried The experience of fear about the future. Fearing that soon something bad might happen or that something good will not.

Wrong The experience of guilt and decreased energy resulting from acting out of alignment with the true self.

APPENDIX

Abuse - Any form of expression, which regardless of intention, transmits a message of limitation which reduces another's sense of self and in turn their self-expression. There is a continuum of abuse. At one end are thoughts and feelings and behaviors that are very subtle but effective. Things like sarcastic verbal put-downs, passive aggressive maneuvers, name calling, ignoring, lying, manipulating, objectifying, and punishing. Things escalate further to violent behaviors like intimidating looks, intentional scares, sudden movements, breaking things, yelling, harassing, and even menacing facial expressions. Then there are the more easily identifiable forms of physical abuse and violence: pushing, shoving, grabbing, spanking, slapping, punching, restraining, raping and killing. All forms of abuse begin as unacknowledged or avoided feelings and eventually manifest as projected neurotic fear. Our tendency to abuse each other is ultimately the result of the contagion of separation that has been passed down through our family histories. See pages 105, 106, 109, 111, 207 & 209.

Archetype - Innate universal symbols that represent ideas or qualities existing within humanity's collective unconscious as well as representing aspects of the individual self. The early 19th century Swiss psychiatrist Carl Jung first introduced the theory. See pages 107, 202 & 219.

Codependency - A defense mechanism which avoids feelings of vulnerability by focusing on the needs of others or one specific other. Rather than connecting with the self and building personal integrity, there is a reliance on other relationships for affirmation and even identity. The codependent says, "I'm okay if you're okay." See pages 111, 112, 152, 231 & 250.

Compassion - Real compassion is connection with the heart of another. The root words are com, "together," and pati, "to suffer." When we are compassionate, we open our heart to become fully aware of the suffering in our friend. Personal empathy is a prerequisite for real compassion because only personal empathy allows us to become self aware to the point that we are capable of offering clean empathy. Real compassion is clean empathy and sympathy working together for the good of all concerned. Real compassion is *healthy compassion* (see sympathy p. 252). We are aware of another's feeling-experience and we are aware of the story attached to the experience. And since our empathy is relatively free of projections, we are able to discern the quality of what is happening before us. This helps us to determine what form of expression our compassion will take. If we feel our friend is sincere and making a concerted effort to improve his situation we may feel compelled to listen or to help. If our friend is confused and projecting or not making a sincere effort to improve his situation, the compassionate act will most likely be to set a boundary. Our compassionate heart connects with the heart of our friend but our friends heart has not yet fully opened, so we find ways to support them in its opening. Compassion is always loving and kind, but healthy compassion will not always appear loving and kind to those who appear to be in need.

Conversely, unhealthy compassion involves empathy and sympathy working together, too, but the phenomenon of projection is also well at work. We may be in denial of ways that we ourselves are suffering and instead direct our energies toward relieving the suffering of the other. We may be unconscious of our lack of love for ourselves and attempt to secure the love of the other by fostering dependency. We might project our guilt onto another's blame in an unconscious attempt to atone or punish ourselves for ways we have abandoned or avoided our self. We may even compensate for unconscious inferiority by taking satisfaction in self-aggrandized superiority. The possibilities are endless, but unhealthy compassion will ultimately feel awkward and draining for everyone involved. Unhealthy compassion compromises personal integrity and perpetuates codependency. In the long run, ironically, unhealthy compassion perpetuates suffering. See pages 78, 120, 127, 191, 193, 202, 204, 210, 218, 231, 245, 246, & 252.

Conscious Anger - Anger used mindfully to communicate boundaries in one's life and restore a legitimate feeling of empowerment within the self. It is not reactive. It is responsive. It is the ability to conjure emotional intensity in order to maintain personal integrity in challenging situations. Once balance is restored the anger completely subsides. See page 125.

Contagion of Separation - Thoughts and feelings of seperation, from others and from the self, are contagious. When we spend time immersed in environments or cultures where feeling separate and without empathy is the norm, we become like the boiling frog who doesn't notice the temperature that is slowly rising. We don't realize the change that is taking place over time and slowly but surely, to some degree, lose our sensitivity and our capacity for empathy. This is especially true for us as children in regard to the different environments we grew up in. See page 113. See also Seperation, pages 166, 167, 194 & 237.

Deflection - An effort to divert one's own attention or the attention of another away from the feeling-topic at hand. Avoidance via distraction. See pages 150 & 157.

Free Association - A mental process first created by Sigmund Freud to help patients overcome unconscious resistance. Patients were presented with a word or image and encouraged to immediately expresses the first idea that entered their mind. Iphelia utilizes free association by focusing on what she is feeling, visualizing a detailed impression of her experience, and then drawing or painting whatever enters her mind. See pages 107 & 229.

Gallows Humor - A defense mechanism that suppresses vulnerable feeling-energy by using humor to dissociate. This is often accomplished by diverting one's attention, focusing on and exaggerating some small aspect of an experience in which humor is found, or by focusing on some other humorous experience from memory or fantasy and completely dissociating from and ignoring the source of the vulnerable feeling. See page 150.

Gaslighting - A defense mechanism which suppresses vulnerable feeling-energy by creating a false experience of power and control. Gaslighting is when a person attempts to manipulate or disorient another person by lying, misdirecting, contradicting, distracting, surprising, or bullying in some covert way. The perpetrator will often attempt to write off the experience as sarcasm or making a joke. Gaslighting is driven by pervasive feelings of inferiority or insecurity which stem from unacknowledged wounds from the past; in other words, unfinished feelings of shame and fear. See page 150.

Inner Guidance Fear - Healthy intuitive fear. It is feeling-guidance which lets us know we are getting off track from ourselves in our decision making. At first this fear may register as a low-grade, background-anxiety, but the longer we ignore the feeling while instead continuing down the unwanted path, the stronger the fear becomes. Noticing and responding to inner guidance fear begins to ensue naturally after we have practiced allowing and observing our natural cycle of emotion. Discerning healthy inner guidance fear from neurotic fear is a continual challenge that requires courage and radical self-honesty. See page 129.

Iphelia - Iphelia's name is derived from the name Ophelia. Ophelia means *to know* and to be like a serpent. It is the name of a character from William Shakespeare's play *Hamlet*. Shakespeare's Ophelia was sensitive and emotionally repressed. She felt torn between the wills of her father and brother and her potential husband, Hamlet. She wasn't able to know for herself what to do and she wasn't able to set boundaries with those who were invading her. Like Ophelia, Iphelia is sensitive and through the course of her story struggles with boundaries. Iphelia learns early on to value and celebrate her sensitivity and later learns to set healthy boundaries with the pushy people in her life. Iphelia's story is not a tragedy. It is a victory. Iphelia is pronounced I-feel-ya. "I-feel-ya" is a statement. It means to empathize, to know the experience of another. Her name is a kind of affirmation. Speaking the name inherently sets an intention. It says, "I now allot a portion of my awareness for you. I am aware of your experience."

Iphelia Moment - Any moment of choice when we become aware of the challenge to be true to the self, either in the world or even within our own inner dialogue. Iphelia moments will usually require some degree of courage to face some degree of fear. See pages 157, 158, 169, 177-194, 202 & 226.

Intellectualising - A defense mechanism that suppresses feeling-energy by emphasizing intellectual understanding of some given matter. This is often accomplished by conjuring an exalted feeling of righteousness which drowns out the more vulnerable feelings of fear, hurt, or sadness. There is the unconscious assumption that since a logically sound and reasonable conclusion has been conceived, the feelings are invalid and should be discarded. See page 150.

Healing Empath - A feeling person who has reached a point in introspection where they (1) have realized and aspire to observe and resolve their tendency to project, (2) take responsibility for their feeling-state and work to develop personal integrity and improve their life to be a better-feeling place, and (3) have learned and accepted the truth that they must be working to heal the self in order to develop the capacity to offer clean empathy and be a healing presence in the lives of others. See pages 119-121.

Healthy Fear - Fear that helps us survive and thrive. Fear of what puts us in danger and fear of what choices might prevent us from reaching the experiences we are seeking. See pages 128, 142, 165, 220 & 232.

Healthy Release of Anger - Anger discharged from the body without causing harm to the self or others and returning the nervous system to a balanced state of empowerment. See pages 124, 126 & 202.

Lizard Brain - One of the oldest regions of the brain known as the amygdala, consisting of two almond shaped organs call amygdalae. The amygdalae are in charge of survival drives like anger, fear, and sexual desire. Fearful memories are also thought to be stored in synaptic networks connecting to the amygdalae. Many of these networks may hold the physical structure of our neurotic fear. See pages 124, 183, 217 & 219.

Malingering - A defense mechanism which suppresses more vulnerable feelings of fear and/or powerlessness via manipulation and control by pretending to be injured or ill, or exaggerating symptoms of an actual injury or illness. See page 150.

Narcissism - In its purity, narcissism is the ultimate process addiction. There is a pattern of constant pursual of gratification through self-aggrandisement as a means to compensate for or avoid deep-seated feelings of shame and inferiority. The narcissistic self is the epitome of consistent emotional suppression over time. Value becomes less and less determined by feeling-guidance from the heart and instead is determined by what can be constructed in the head—what fits with the grandiose story. There is no capacity for empathy because the attention is always busy serving a self-created ego-driven delusion. Vulnerable feelings are continually suppressed. There is no humility because there isn't the sensitivity to be aware of any real context outside of the delusional story. The narcissistic self is usually preoccupied with how he is perceived by others and at his worst he is constantly reassuring himself of his superiority while projecting all of his inferiority and shame onto the world around him. See pages 112, 217 & 225.

Natural Cycle of Emotion - How our emotional bodies are supposed to operate. Feeling what we feel, when we feel it. We allow the emotional energy within the body to move without any will to suppress. In the beginning, for most, this will require a mindful effort to suspend all the avoidance patterns and defense mechanisms that have been developed for years. As we develop our mature adult self we find healthy productive ways to allow the natural cycle of emotion to flow, which are beneficial to ourselves, our families, our communities, and in turn, the whole world. See pages 123, 132, 150, 165, 208, 225, 226 & 248.

Neurotic Fear - An old fear projected onto current circumstances, which is resulting from unfinished feelings or trauma from the past. There is a need to completely feel all of one's anger or sadness around a past experience. Then there can be the release of the past and/or the restoring of power that was lost. See pages 129, 135, 165, 166, 180, 194, 216, 222, 233, 241, 246 & 247.

Resistance - The experience of any number of active defense mechanisms which unconsciously or indirectly oppose the natural flow of emotion and/or authentic expression of self. Resistance refuses the call toward integration and wholeness for the individual and avoids intimacy and real connection in relationship. See pages 108, 146, 189, 202 & 247.

Sarcasm - Passive aggressive expression using humor to cover other more vulnerable feelings like anger, fear, hurt, or sadness. Some forms of sarcasm often manifest as gaslighting and are therefore abusive. See pages 150, 216 & 248.

Secondary Anger - A defense mechanism that conjures powerful emotional intensity in an effort to suppress or avoid a feeling of fear which is often fear of more vulnerable feelings of guilt, shame, hurt, or sadness. See pages 123, 124, 130, 189, 219 & 233.

Shadow - The parts of our self we choose to dissociate from and suppress. We are unconscious of our shadow parts but there is usually evidence of them in what we judge or are viscerally repulsed by in others. The shadow parts of our psyche are what we suppress and don't believe ourselves to be, but ironically, contain resources the rest of our being needs to be whole and realize its fullest potential. See pages 119 & 210.

Spiritual Bypass - Using spiritual ideas and practices to avoid feelings of vulnerability like guilt, shame, hurt, sadness, fear, and especially anger. There are infinite examples. Things like regularly confessing sins without making any effort to change the behavior, meditating all day and avoiding life, over-emphasising the positive, anger avoidance because one should always be "compassionate," preoccupation with phenomena of spiritual experience, or making lofty blanketing statements like, "It's all an illusion anyway," or "It was meant to be," to avoid feeling vulnerable. Spiritual bypass is not spiritual. See page 150.

Sympathy - An experience of empathy which includes some degree of projection. Our personal story is in some way resonating with what we perceive before us and we are more likely to agree with the story being told. Empathy is our capacity to be aware of what another is experiencing, which validates that person's feelings but not necessarily the meaning of the content to which the feeling-experience is connected. Often sympathy means that we validate more that just the experience. We are to some degree agreeing with the story that generates the experience. We have to be careful with sympathy because a person's story can often keep them stuck feeling depressed and powerless, or angry and justified. There are infinite ways to rationalize avoiding our unfinished business. And sometimes sympathy can pull us into a drama that is not ours to begin with—a classic pitfall for the codependent wounded empath! Clean empathy validates feelings but is more concerned with the broader meaning of the story's content for an individual. How does the story instigate growth for the individual? What is the growth task or challenge inherent in the story? What is the courageous path to empowerment for the individual? These are all questions that arise when we listen with an open heart. See page 207.

True Conscience - Emotional feedback helping us evaluate our thoughts, words, and behaviors. Rather than being developed by internalizing social norms, the true conscience is instead arrived at in the present moment via feeling-guidance sensed from deep within the heart. From the heart we can sense and know what feels right and good and true; what is harmonious and beneficial to nature, our family, friends, and the whole of humanity. From deep within the heart we can feel a universal love flowing to and through and animating all things. This feeling of unconditional love is the light helping us see what thoughts, words, and behaviors are true to our individual nature. See page 145.

True Self - The experience of the self accompanied by feelings of exhilaration. When we act in accordance with the deeper feeling-guidance from within, there is energy and a feeling of being free. More the maintaining of a collection and steady direction than any kind of arrival, identifying the true self is a continual process of discovery. The practice of personal integrity can lead to ever heightened experiences of the self, both in consciousness and through expression in the world. See pages 119, 120, 129, 131, 143, 145, 146, 158, 159, 182, 199, 203, 207, 209, 225, 226, 230, 234, 235 & 237-242.

Validation - All feelings are valid. They are real and they happen. Everyone's experience is valid, even when it is not the same as ours. But sometimes it may seem like someone is having feelings about an experience that do not make sense to us. This may be because they are projecting the dream of an old undigested experience onto the current circumstances. It is also possible that we are projecting an old undigested experience onto the experience of their expression. In most instances both are happening to a greater or lesser degree. In any case, especially with children, it is always important to validate their experience lest they learn to ignore their feelings. See pages 1, 25 & 252.

There is a level of experience beyond what our physical senses can detect. Whether we are conscious of it or not, this is the level from which we are simultaneously perceiving and creating our world. To become aware of this level of experience we have to be sensitive and pay attention. We have to experiment and learn its truths, its rules, and its boundaries. The inherent

incentive for paying attention is that we can improve our experience. We can reach upward and aspire toward a better-feeling place. Then there is no need for avoidance, suppression, or addiction. This ever-better-feeling place exists for us all. And finding it for ourselves supports everyone else in their discovery. We are one. *And* we are free. A mysterious and extrodinary gift. A gift of feeling.

Erick Kenneth French is a Licensed Clinical Social Worker and Advanced Clinical Hypnotherapist. He has been studying and training at the Wellness Institute in Issaquah, Washington, for the past seven years. He is the founder of One Awareness Counseling in Saint Louis, Missouri, where he has maintained a thriving private practice for the past 11 years. He regularly facilitates five-weekend personal transformation retreats that incorporate a multitude of healing modalities including hypnotherapy, breathwork, and meditation. Erick teaches that spiritual awakening begins with paying attention to and successfully receiving the messages of feelings, and that restoring and retaining our capacity for empathy is critical to personal fulfillment and, ultimately, the survival of humanity.

For more information about Erick visit:
www.OneAwarenessCounseling.com

Awaken the Gift of Feeling
www.Iphelia.com
f Iphelia
🐦 IpheliaBook

Connect with community and join the discussion!
Visit: forum.Iphelia.com

TYRIAN PRESS

Coming soon from Tyrian Press!

Iphelia: Awakening the Gift of Feeling, Children's Edition, is the graphic novel from the original presented in a larger 8 x 10 hardback which includes 110 pages of high quality digital offset printed images, delivering more detail with more vivid color. The perfect gift for children and those with a special appreciation for the digital artwork of Iphelia.

This book was made to help children retain their capacity for empathy, and to help adults remember theirs.

For more information visit:
www.TyrianPress.com
www.Iphelia.com

CPSIA information can be obtained
at www.ICGtesting.com
Printed in the USA
BVOW11s0740310717

490694BV00013B/118/P